MAGNOLIA JOURNEY

Southern Historical Publications No. 17

MAGNOLIA JOURNEY

A UNION VETERAN REVISITS THE FORMER CONFEDERATE STATES

Arranged from Letters of Correspondent Russell H. Conwell

to the *Daily Evening Traveller* (Boston, 1869)

By

Joseph C. Carter

The University of Alabama Press

University, Alabama

547601

PREFACE

A national magazine recently carried a reminiscent article by Paul E. Deutschman titled "A GI Returns to the Great Battle Areas of Europe." Later, some daily newspapers released a serial article, "D-Day Plus 20," in which General Dwight D. Eisenhower narrated his visit to the World War II invasion sites along the Normandy Coast two decades after that famous day. But Americans also have participated in other great wars where their blood has been shed at the fields and forts of freedom.

A century ago—in 1869—Russell H. Conwell, a New England reporter and Union Army veteran, then only twenty-six, visited many of the battle sites of the Civil War and wrote under the penname of "Russell," a series of twenty-five "letters" which were published that year in the *Daily Evening Traveller*, a Boston newspaper. The letters (today they would be called feature articles) described sites of the war that had ended only four years before. All except one of the letters were titled "Battle-Fields of the Rebellion." That one, apparently because of lack of editorial foresight, was published under the title "Battle-Fields of Virginia." Yet the editors of the *Traveller*, from the start, undoubtedly had intended to make the series one coordinated post-Civil War feature.

Eleven of the twenty-five letters were published with datelines as follows: Gordonville, Va., March 10; Richmond, Va., March 27; Petersburg, Va., March 31; Written on a Stump Near Williamsburg, Va., April 8; Newbern, N.C., April 15; Charleston, S.C., April 20; Macon, Ga., April 26; New Orleans, La., May 3; Vicksburg[Miss.], May 12; Nashville, Tenn., May 17; and Harper's Ferry, W.Va., May 27. The other fourteen letters were not datelined, at least not in print.

The letters were published by the *Traveller* in its issues dated March 18 and 30; April 6, 13, 20, and 27; May 4, 11, 18, and 25; June 1, 8, 15, 22,

v

and 29; July 6, 13, 20, and 27; August 3, 10, 17, 24, and 31; and September 7. All were Tuesday editions except the first one,which was dated Thursday. A special editorial letter titled "The National Dead," written by Conwell to refute false charges against the Burial Corps,was published in the same newspaper September 21, but is not included in this volume.

The order in which the articles first appeared in the Boston newspaper has been changed herein to conform (as accurately as can be ascertained) to the itinerary of battlefields, forts, cemeteries, and other localities visited by Conwell during his "grand tour" of ten of the eleven former Confederate States: Alabama, Arkansas, Florida, Georgia, Louisiana, Mississippi, North Carolina, South Carolina, Tennessee, and Virginia. He omitted only Texas during his three-months' reportorial tour through the South, probably because Texas had had no major battles during the recent war. The arrangement herein of the subdivisions of the original twenty-five long articles into seventy-four shorter segments is intended both to accommodate the reader and to highlight the topographic variety and profusion of Conwell's journey. A correlation between these segments and the original newspaper articles is given in the Table of Contents, by showing, in parentheses following the caption of each segment, the serial number of the original article(s) in which the segment appeared.

In an editorial notice promoting the article series about to be written by Conwell,Publisher Roland Worthington (of Worthington, Flanders & Co., 31 State Street, Boston) announced that the *Traveller* would "spare no expense in making this feature of the paper all our patrons can wish," and added that Russell Conwell, "being regularly attached to the *Traveller* corps,will spare no pains in gathering interesting information." Then, when he had completed the series,Conwell wrote, in the modest manner of any good newspaperman who had tried to do his duty, "What we have done or written is nothing more than what the editors of the *Traveller* sent us to do, and to them be all the thanks if there are any."

Conwell had been living in Somerville (a suburb

of Boston) since the year before, having returned from Minnesota to his native Massachusetts with his wife, Jennie. The preceding two years he had been a newspaperman in Minneapolis, had toured some of the famous battlefields of Europe, and had visited Palestine. An 1865 graduate of Albany Law School, he also had practiced law a year or so in the Minneapolis-St. Paul area before engaging in journalism.

Today's traveling correspondent would carry a tape recorder, a typewriter, or both—but at least a pocket full of copy paper. Conwell in 1869 equipped himself with what he described as a "diary" onto whose pages he wrote what he saw and heard and thought. In fact, at one point in his travels through the Deep South he commented: "God bless the man that invented diaries! They are the only preventative now in use to keep wandering correspondents from insanity. Even with them we feel as if life was only a 'lucid interval' so strangely and inconsistently are the evils and virtues, pleasures and pains of life jumbled together in the experience of a Northern man who visits and observes the people of the South."

Since neither typewriters nor telephones were then in use, he undoubtedly penned his articles in longhand and mailed them to his newspaper to be set slowly into type by hand in the manner of printers of that pre-Linotype era. Today's news correspondent speeds from scene to scene by railroad, automobile, helicopter, or jet. But Russell Conwell's tour of historic sites and towns was accomplished by slower, more primitive means. He probably traveled from Boston to Washington by train. Through parts of eastern Virginia he rode a two-wheeled farm cart drawn by a mule and driven by a girl. Later he took "the cars" but soon found a cow cart useful; later, a spirited pony; and again, a mule driver.

In coastal North Carolina he rode a river tugboat, was carried on the back of a Negro boatman, traveled by river steamer, and used a row boat. In South Carolina a steamboat and later some horses were his modes of transportation. Elsewhere in South Carolina, and in Georgia, Florida, Alabama, and Louisiana, he moved about by railroad. He sailed up the Mississippi River and some of its tributaries on a paddlewheel steamer. In parts of Tennessee and western Georgia, he again drove mule teams; and in Northern Virginia and Maryland the roving newspaperman added teams of livery horses to his list of travel means.

Conwell's articles picturing the conditions of the battlefields of the War of the Rebellion are written almost entirely in the first person plural style then common among newspaper writers—especially those who wrote features or editorials. However, in spite of the plural implications of his pronouns—"we," "us," "our," and "our"—he traveled alone except on a few occasions where he clearly states he had a local guide to show him about.

His articles contain much fine narration, many rich descriptions, and keen sociological observations. His sly wit, his amusing anecdotes, his rich vocabulary, and his knowledge of military events, history, and literature reflect many of the great classics of American, British, Latin, and Greek literatures. These he had studied in his childhood home at Worthington, Massachusetts; in the Academy at Wilbraham, Massachusetts; and in Yale College at New Haven, Connecticut. In these articles the scholarly young writer quotes aptly from more than three dozen early authors and from the King James version of the Bible.

Conwell must have been a voracious reader with an unusually retentive memory for names, quotations, technical facts, and figures of speech. It is doubtful if he was able, during his assigned tour, to take time to rewrite his articles; so it is amazing that many of them attain such heights of literary excellence. His range of interests was broad and his style sometimes light and lyrical, yet at other times earthy and pointed in its punch. His enthusiasm, his commentaries on people and events, and his keen observation of details all combine to make him what editors today would call a talented feature writer.

These articles, written during the first decade of the nation's Reconstruction Era, comprise an exciting and historically valuable description of many of America's military fields, forts, cemeteries, and civilian areas as they were seen by a newspaper reporter a century ago. The United States of that time—at least much of the area east of the Mississippi River—lives again in these *Traveller* essays, and many of the battles of the War between the States are fought again in all their fury. Also, although Russell Conwell was then only twenty-six, life already had matured him so that he was able to advise his *Traveller* readers sagely: "How important...for a student of history to visit localities in order to get a fair understanding of the events about which he reads." Nearly all the places that young correspondent visited, I included also in two of my own tours of the South as part of the editorial research on these articles.

Some of Conwell's remarks as he describes people and scenes reflect the same postwar bitterness that very likely existed in the hearts of many other Union veterans toward the people of the former Confederate States, whose military forces had been defeated after four years of bloody, fratricidal war. Young Conwell's assignment from the editor of the *Traveller* was quite timely, and reader interest in his series must have been brisk, indeed; for six of the states which had seceded from the United States had been readmitted to the Union only the year before under the Reconstruction Act of 1867. Tennessee had come back in 1866, the first to return. Four states—Georgia, Mississippi, Texas, and Virginia—were still "in limbo," being, administered by army commanders in military districts. They were not readmitted until 1870. Some of Conwell's bitterness and accompanying sarcasms (probably not unlike that of many newspapermen of that painful era) shows particularly through the lines telling of his interviews with Generals Pierre Beauregard and Nathan Forrest, and his brief glimpse of General Jubal Early.

Conwell had served as a captain—first of infantry, then of heavy artillery—in North Carolina and Virginia and, during his service years (1862-1864), had visited more informally other war sectors in Tennessee and Georgia. So in part his travels while writing these articles were a sentimental journey back to some of the scenes that he already knew quite well.

A few years after publication of this series in

the *Traveller*, Russell Conwell left journalism as an active career (although he taught news reporting later as a college professor); practiced law again (this time in Boston); and became a Lyceum and Chautauqua lecturer, an ordained clergyman (serving Baptist churches in Lexington, Massachusetts, and Philadelphia, Pennsylvania and later founder and first president of Temple University. He was also the author of several books. Today, despite his fruitful work as a preacher and educator, Conwell is probably most widely remembered for his many public orations, especially the world famous "Acres of Diamonds," which he delivered several thousand times, with variations of structure, to enraptured audiences here and abroad.

In editing these letters for accuracy, clarity, and reader appeal, I have employed standard maps, official documents and reports, and other reliable reference sources, both primary and secondary. The word "Negro" I have capitalized throughout, although the *Traveller* (as did most publications of 1869— and many even much later) printed it in lower case as "negro." In a few spots I have found it necessary to smooth out punctuation where it deviated radically from present standards. But otherwise the style and content of Conwell's original correspondence have been faithfully retained, although compacted somewhat for space.

Words in brackets are mine (not Conwell's) and were inserted to complete factual statements or to clarify their meanings. Quotation marks that appear in the text are Conwell's; I have added no others.

All of "Russell's Letters" are presented in this volume with the gracious permission of Robert Choate, editor and publisher of the Boston Herald-Traveler Corporation. The generosity of Mr. Choate and the Corporation is gratefully acknowledged.

My thanks also are extended to two Temple University colleagues, Professors Harry M. Tinkcom of the History Department and R. Bruce Underwood of the Journalism Department, both of whom carefully read the completed manuscript and provided much helpful encouragement toward its publication.

Joseph C. Carter

Philadelphia, Pa.
October, 1973

CONTENTS

MAGNOLIA JOURNEY

AROUND WASHINGTON

Around Washington!   What visions of camp life,
with all its vexations and pleasures,come back with
these two words! Those days of hard work with the
spade upon forts; dress parades and brigade drills;
and feverish days in the hospital. Around Washington! That city for whose defense so many brave men
died. That city full of traitors who lost no op-
portunity to aid the rebellion. That city which,
but for its being the capital of the Republic, would
have been burned to ashes long ago.

Five years ago it was a city of war. The flags
on fort and camp dimmed the sunlight in every direction. Its streets were filled with officers and
soldiers; hospital and guard tents lined its avenues;   while from its storehouses streamed long
trains of army wagons blocking each outlet of the
city with their cumbrous wheels.

A military city,so full of uniforms that a citizen's dress appeared strange and awkward. So full
of mule teams and ammunition trains that a private
carriage was a novelty. Even the dignified senators and blustering representatives were swallowed
up in the military crowd, and appeared most singularly out of place in citizen's clothes.

"We want men to garrison the forts around Washington," said the recruiting officers [early] in
1864; and how many a fond mother let her son go to
the "easy service" of garrisoning Washington, and
in a few months heard of his death [outside Fredericksburg, May 5-6, 1864] on the battlefield of
the Wilderness.

"We want men to defend Washington," said they
earlier in the war; and the troops raised for that
purpose filled thê valleys and covered the hills of
Tennessee, Louisiana, and the Carolinas.

"To defend Washington!" How it stirred the hearts
of patriots to think that the Capitol was in danger. How much indebted did the people of the North
feel to General [Benjamin F.]Butler for his prompt-
ness in moving on his own responsibility to the de-

1

fense of Washington. Whether the national government would have been able to hold the city against
the host of traitors within its precincts had any
other less decided character than Butler been ordered to its defense is a question for historical
philosophers.

How does it appear today? It is a very different city from the Washington of war time—which is
saying but little for its credit. Take away the
government buildings and it would be one of the most
dreary, desolate cities in the world. Not but that
its avenues are wide enough, and its buildings large
enough, for they are spacious and convenient. But
their dull and tenantless appearance during the "va-
cation" of Congress and their "hanger-on" appearance when Congress is in session give to the stranger the impression of a great burlesque.

The forts in which the soldier did his duty, and
upon whose strength officials relied for the safety of the city, are now going fast to nature's level [in their former ring around the city.] Little
mounds are all that can be seen of some; others
have disappeared. Forts Worth, Ward, Blinker, Rich-
ardson, Scott, Runyon, Albany, Jackson, Craig, Til-
linghast, Cass, DeKalb, Corcoran, Bennett, Ethan
Allen, Marcy, Gaines, Pennsylvania, Vermont [a bat-
tery], Slocum, Massachusetts, Totten, Slemmer, Bunk-
er Hill, Saratoga, Thayer, Lincoln, Mahan, Baker,
Davis, Wagner, Stanton, Snyder, Carroll, Greble,
Ellsworth, and Lyon are fast sinking into oblivion.

Gone forever the games at cards, letters from home,
boxes of clothing, pass days to the city, camp stories and scenes—bright spots in the dark days of
war and recalled with pleasure. The great parades,
national salutes, parks of artillery, squadrons of
cavalry, signal stations, and flags that waved over
camps and buildings are gone, too, with the days of
'64.

If the officers and soldiers who garrisoned Georgetown Heights were to return today, they would be in
a quandary as to the location of their old quarters.
The redoubts and lines of rifle-pits have been dug
away, and in many places the hills upon which the
works were located have shared the same fate; and
today the carpenters and masons "make merry" upon

the residences which are being constructed along
the heights for wealthy men. In fact these heights
are now becoming most fashionable for the residences
of the rich, and many who have heretofore lived down
in the city of Georgetown, or in the suburbs of
Washington, are removing to this spot.

Probably no landmark in or about Washington is
more familiar to the soldiers than Long Bridge. Few
indeed were the regiments that did not cross it,
and fewer still the soldiers who did not wish it
less than half as long. [It was about one and a
half miles in length.] But it has grown weak since
the military arm which built it has relinquished
the care of it, and now it is declared unsafe for
railway travel. The highway, however, is kept open,
and all kinds of teams can be seen constantly crossing to and fro every hour. But the gunboats the
soldiers saw from it, the heavy-laden supply ships,
the scows and pontoons have entirely disappeared;
and a calm [Potomac] river, that flows on in peace,
spreads its shining sheet before the visitor, un-
torn by the paddles of transports or the screws of
iron-clads.

But the graves are left with all their sad reminiscences; and Arlington Heights, once the beautiful residence of General Robert E. Lee, is now
one great graveyard. [Arlington National Cemetery,
established 1864.] The grand old mansion [the Cus-
tis-Lee home, formerly called "Arlington House"] with
its barns and Negro quarters is occupied by the
keeper of the cemetery, and its massive doors are
always open to those who visit the spot. But from
its very doorway, stretching far down the hillside,
are the graves of Union soldiers [the first buried
in 1864]. It was a beautiful location before the
war, and its beauty has been greatly increased by
the new paths, new trees and lawns which now adorn
the cemetery. [The historical background of both
the Lee Mansion and Arlington Cemetery are richly
detailed in Myrtle C. Murdock's book, *Your Memor-
ials in Washington* (Washington: Monumental Press,
1952), pp. 61-96.]

From this elevation the visitor can look down upon Washington and Georgetown, the winding waters of
the Potomac, and the undulating hills of the East
Branch [now called the Anacostia] Valley. Here sat

General Lee in 1861,surrounded by every luxury of life,and from this porch gazed upon the city,saying it should be destroyed. Had any one said that his lands should be taken, the grounds about his house used for a graveyard, his barns be taken as a storehouse for Yankee coffins,and his mansion for offices and sexton's quarters,while his own slaves would be hired to decorate the graves of his enemies, he would have considered it impossible.

But the magician of war has pronounced his *Presto*! and Lee is an exile[and president of Washington College],and the halls his family used to love now echo to the tread of different feet. [He left the property early in the war when he resigned his United States Army commission.] Its parlors with their army portraits and cemetery views have a more modern look than the old-fashioned portraits of the Lee family [and one might muse with Thomas Moore]

The smiles, the tears of boyhood's years,
The words of love then spoken,
The eyes that shone now dimm'd and gone,
The cheerful hearts now broken.
I feel like one who treads alone
Some banquet hall deserted,
Whose lights are fled, whose garlands dead,
And all but me departed.

It was intimated to us by some half-rebels that these bodies would be taken up by the government and interred somewhere else. For,without a violation of the Constitution, Congress cannot pass a "bill of attainder" which prevents the children from coming into possession of the property. Congress can confiscate property only during the life of its owner, after which it must revert to the heirs. [The 1100 acre Lee estate was seized by the Federal government in 1864.] If such is the case, when Lee dies his heirs can,and doubtless will,come to claim their own, and the government will be obliged either to relinquish it or pay any sum,no matter how great, which the heirs demand for it. [The sum of $150,000 was paid to Lee's son George in 1883.]

It seems like shortsightedness on the part of the Quartermaster General to take this estate for a cemetery. Our informant stated that this was the case with the cemeteries at Richmond and Hampton [also in Virginia], and in many other places. It is a bad job, if, after ten or twelve years, all these bodies must be removed because the children of the former owners come to claim the land. We had hoped that the bones of these heroes might be permitted now to rest forever in peace, and that another removal might not be cited as a sample of the "ungratefulness of republics." [Apparently Conwell remembered the phrase, inexactly, from Niccolo Machiavelli's *Discourses on the First Ten Books of Livy*. In Discourse I, chapter 30, "ingratitude" is called a vice of republics. The lamentation also was later expressed (concerning Thomas Jefferson's monument) in Edward King's *The Southern States of North America* (London: Blackie & Son, 1875), p. 653.]

From Arlington Heights we went to Alexandria. But the change here since the war, except in uniforms, has not been sufficiently marked to permit us to dwell long upon it. The streets have that same "Virginia look" which they had during the war, and the houses and the stores appear just about as gloomy. In the barroom of the Marshall House, where [Union Army Colonel Elmer E] Ellsworth was killed [May 24, 1861, for pulling down a Confederate flag], we saw a long-haired Virginian boasting how he loved [James] Jackson, the former proprietor, and how willing he would be to go North (for three drinks) and avenge Jackson's death. The house seems to be patronized well by Southerners and by Confederacy-loving young ladies who deem it a great honor to stand under the same roof where fell the "martyr Jackson" [killed by Ellsworth's corporal]. It has at present, however, passed out of the hands of the Jackson family and is kept by a man who boasts that he is "neither one thing nor another."

Alexandria has never been reconstructed. Its inhabitants [in 1869] are as bitter enemies of the nation as they ever were, and their acts and words in any other land would bring hundreds of them to the gallows. Portraits of Jeff Davis and Lee hang in all their parlors, decorated with Confederate flags. Photographs of [John] Wilkes Booth, with the last words of great martyrs printed upon its borders; effigies of Abraham Lincoln hanging by the neck with a darkey hung at each heel, together with Confederate songs, mottoes, and keepsakes, adorn their drawing-rooms. They shun or insult men who have been National soldiers and shower their favors upon Confederates. They keep the graves in the Confederate cemetery decorated with flowers, and by word and look expel every Northerner that they know to be within its gates. To be a lion in Alexandria one has only to be a Confederate soldier; the mothers shower their blessings upon him; fathers share their meals with him; brothers extend a cordial welcome; sisters kiss and hug him; and everybody praises his beauty and intelligence. A Union soldier is to them a vagabond and outcast, a wolf in sheep's clothing, and everything contemptible and bad.

This same Alexandria, which was the first to raise the Confederate flag in Virginia, is also the last to lay it aside. The forts around have been washed away, and even the great redoubts near the Fairfax [Episcopal Theological] Seminary have been obliterated by the plough; but the rebellion, which they were erected to subdue, seems not to be dead yet. Poor people! we pity them—harassed as they are by disappointment, hatred, avarice, selfishness, and pride.

FREDERICKSBURG

Since we began our trip through Virginia an old poem, recited in our boyhood days, has been constantly ringing in our ears:

> New England's dead! New England's dead!
> On every hill they lie;
> On every field of strife made red
> By bloody victory.

[McLellan, Isaac, Jr., "New England's Dead," a 19th century school-reader classic, in Edmund C. Stedman's *An American Anthology: 1787-1900* (Boston: Houghton Mifflin Co., 1900), p. 190.]

As if written in the spirit of prophecy, these lines contain much more truth to-day than when they first saw the [printing] type.

What thoughts or emotions may be awakened in the mind of the civilian, as he treads in the footsteps of those armies whose sacrifices make the soil of Virginia sacred, we cannot tell. But to a soldier —who is reminded at every turn of the fatiguing marches, chilly and sleepless nights, fierce combat and dying comrades—there is a charm about the dilapidated rifle pits and scarred trees which clothes them with a fascinating interest. Even the sticky, sloppy, copper-colored mud contains a volume of unwritten history.

Great changes have come over Virginia since the days of '62. They who then looked from the mountain top over the forests, large plantations, and thriving cities with smiles of satisfaction and pride must to-day contemplate its shattered and ruined state with sadness and tears. War has transformed the "Garden of the South" into the "Graveyard of America," and Prince [Francois] de Joinville [a French exile who served in the Union army under General George B. McClellan] used apt words when he said, "Virginia should be enclosed with a high fence and kept sacred as the Cemetery of the War." For, after all the removals, at least a hundred and fifty thousand dead lie undisturbed beneath the soil of her battlefields. The National Government has done much toward gathering them up and has buried them carefully in the several National cemeteries. But scarcely a day passes when the plough of the farmer tilling the soil, or the spade of the Negro hunting lead, does not disturb in their secret resting-places the bones of Union soldiers. The Confederate dead, falling in close proximity to their homes or the residences of friends, were gathered up and buried in their own public cemeteries.

The earthworks, which so distinguished our army in the early part of the campaign in Virginia, are in some places nearly obliterated—especially at Manassas, Ball's Bluff, Winchester, Cedar Mountain, and the fields near Washington. A stranger to the country, however well he might be acquainted with the history of those early campaigns, could not trace at these places the works of either army, although numerous mounds and pits still remain.

The graves, which at Bull Run were for several

years after the struggle the most interesting and, from their situation on the hill side, the most conspicuous features of the battlefield, have now become empty and are levelled with the earth. But the more recently constructed lines of breastworks used in the battles of the Wilderness, Fredericksburg, Fair Oaks, Williamsburg, and Petersburg are still almost entire.

Two days cannot better be expended by the traveller—be he soldier or civilian—than in walking over the fortifications which surround Fredericksburg. Every foot of land for miles around is full of interest. The roofless houses, blackened walls, bullet- and shell-perforated buildings in the city, with the beautiful National Cemetery, and the rebel fortifications on Marye's Heights, give to the historian or novelist standing on the Falmouth side of the Rappahannock a sample of an ideal battlefield.

The valley in which the city stands is of half-moon shape and hemmed in by a circular range of steep hills, reaching from the river about half a mile below the city, around to the river again about two miles above. On this range of hills, which so effectually enclosed the city, the rebels erected their batteries and rifle-pits. The land on the Falmouth side of the Rappahanock, and opposite the city, rises abruptly to a great elevation [Stafford Heights] and here were planted the heavy guns of the Union army on that fatal December day [Saturday the 13th, 1862] when the Army of the Potomac, under General [Ambrose] Burnside, attempted to drive the rebels [commanded by General Lee] from their strong position. From the high ground occupied by our troops across to the encircling [Marye's] Heights, fortified by the rebels, was an easy range for heavy artillery, and the marks of the huge missiles can still be seen in the earth on either side.

The unthrifty city has remained in *status quo* since the war, and it is nearly as easy now to follow the steps of our brave boys who went to defeat under Burnside in December, '62, and to a glorious victory [there against Confederate General Jubal Early] under [Union General John] Sedgwick in May, '63, as it was immediately after those battles. The partially burned pontoons over which so many of old

Massachusetts' sons went to certain death still obstruct navigation. The ruins of warehouses blown up by the rebels, of dwellings and iron works burned by Burnside and Sedgwick stand unchanged in sad desolation. The graves of our soldiers who were buried where they fell (and who have since been removed to the new [National] Cemetery on the heights) are now open, and all along the plain in the rear of the city they threaten to engulf the careless traveller.

The establishment of a National Cemetery is the only material change and as it stands on the hillside [off Lafayette Blvd.] with its beautiful walks and neat rows of graves it presents a striking contrast to the desolation around. In this cemetery, a soldier informed us, lie the remains of Union soldiers who fell at or near Fredericksburg, and out of the 30,000, alas, 15,000 lie beneath simple, white headboards which bear that sad inscription, "Unknown." Two, four, and sometimes eight of these are buried in graves together. As we walked along the gravelled walks and among the shade trees, while the old flag waved as proudly above us as in the days of '63, we could read the names of thousands representing nearly every Northern State, the greater part of whom are there simply because their friends know not where to look for them. One headboard surprised us with an inscription bearing the name of a dear friend, whose parents had spent months of time and a fortune of money vainly endeavoring to find him. The superintendent of the cemetery gave us a brief sketch of the manner in which the dead were buried.

In 1865 the Union dead were scattered about the fields and forests in the vicinity of Fredericksburg. Some were buried, some half buried, and many lay about in the grass and leaves not buried at all. Those who had been interred by their comrades had boards bearing their names placed at the heads of their graves; and, but for the fact that the poor whites and Negroes in a most barbarous manner pulled up the boards and used them for firewood, thousands now marked "Unknown" would have been found by their friends [that is, their families]. However, in some cases an engraved watch, or knife, or letters on the decayed clothing found in the grave would identify them.

In this manner doubtless our friend was identified when removed to the cemetery,although he could not be found before. Whenever the battlefield was left in the possession of the enemy, as was the case after Burnside's disastrous defeat, they dug the graves wherever they found the bodies and threw them carelessly in,leaving no mark to tell who lay there. In many cases they dug long trenches and buried from ten to a hundred in a grave. When these were exhumed to be taken to the cemetery their bones fell to pieces, and it became a necessity to bury several together as they became so mixed. The remains of one could not be distinguished from another and the number taken up could only be told by the number of skulls they found. These graves surrounded us on every hand bearing such inscriptions as:

5
United States
Soldiers
Unknown.

With sorrowful thoughts of the many bereaved family circles of broken hearts,of suffering dependents,we turned from the cemetery gate that day to visit Marye's Heights. Upon this spot the rebels erected their strongest battery. At its foot was the stone wall where stood the rebels whose fire in the December [1862] fight swept off our advancing columns by thousands. It is but a few rods from the cemetery and commands a view of the landscape for several miles around. [John Lawrence] Marye, who owned the land, rebuilt his house three years ago—a large brick structure—but he soon after died and the house is unoccupied. The adjoining buildings, which stood in the time of the battles, are so riddled with bullets as to present the appearance of a sieve.

Here we stood and contemplated the landscape, thinking of the fearful scene when our troops filed down to the opposite side of the river and came across the pontoons into the city under the heavy artillery fire. What a scene must have presented itself to General Lee as he came to Marye's house and saw,with General [James] Longstreet,from this

spot the gallant charge of General [Edwin V.] Sum-
ner's and Gen. [Oliver O.] Howard's divisions—when
the Ninth and Second Corps, though losing the day,
won imperishable honors, and when 2,000 Massachusetts men made their last charge on earth, including heroes from the 1st, 7th, 9th, 10th, 11th, 12th,
13th, 14th [redesignated 1st Heavy Artillery], 15th,
16th, 18th, 19th, 20th, 21st, 22nd, 32nd, 33d, 35th,
36th, and 39th regiments.   How could they stand?
That high stone wall at the foot of the hill could
not be taken. No man could live that stood before
that constant stream of fire.
    There on the plain [Union]   General [George W.]
Getty's troops piled their dead in huge heaps, re-
treated,   came on again—lying behind the breastworks made of human bodies,   battered the pile of
stone with lead. But it was of no use. A position
so strong, so bravely defended, could not be tak-
en. General Burnside was looking at them from the
Lacy House, on the opposite side of the river, and
they were ashamed to fail. But they had to submit.
Old men, wounded and exhausted, forgot their suffering to weep at their own defeat.   [More than
12,000 Union troops were lost.]   But there came a
day when this dishonor was to be expunged; and the
following May [3-4, 1863] General Sedgwick, taking
the enemy nearly by surprise, stormed the same stone
wall, mounted the heights, and drove hence the foe.
Then it was that the 7th and 10th Massachusetts won
some of their greatest laurels by "following Uncle
John" [Sedgwick]. In both of these engagments the
slope and plain were covered with the dead and dying. Many of the dead were buried where they fell.
    In the Confederate Cemetery at [William and Wash-
ington Streets] we found the fence blown over, the
graves of the soldiers were hardly distinguishable,
while in several cases the graves were either never
filled or since dug open, leaving the ends of the
coffins exposed to view.   In one of these graves
was a large yellow dog which snapped and growled at
us in a hideous way from his station on the coffin.
He had dug all around the box and the cover was
slightly ajar. His fierce appearance, however, prevented any extensive investigations.   As we left
the grounds the boys gathered on the walls and threw
stones at him.   A passing citizen stated that the

dog did not belong in Fredericksburg, nor did any one know where he came from or who lay in the grave. But the dog had been there for six months, keeping guard all the while on that coffin. He went away only in the night to get his food and returned at once to his post.

The only supposition which will account for the strange behavior of the dog is, that after two years of search he at last found his master there in that neglected grave, and as if to shame the human race, he began his faithful watch, doing the duty which properly belonged to his master's kind. It would seem that such an instance of faithfulness would at least shame the people into the pains of covering the graves of their "unknown" comrades. It was a wretched graveyard, shattered, worn, and neglected, yet it was proposed in our hearing to erect a monument to the Confederate soldiers there. Sad contrasts between the resting places of the conquerors and the conquered!

From the cemetery we proceeded to the city [Fredericksburg] and endeavored, as far as possible, to learn the sentiments of the people toward the North. Universally did they disclaim any personal hatred of the people of the North, although they keenly felt their defeat. They treated us with that genial courtesy and hospitality in which the Southern people pride themselves, and did all in their power to make our visit pleasant and profitable. Some of those we met in the hotels had done their best but a few years ago to send a bullet to our heart. They greeted us, however, with generous smiles, readily gave us their hands, remarking "Those were right smart warm times," and adding that they were glad such times had passed. They gathered around us, offering us food, drink and shelter, free, and entertained us long with their stories of the war. Few hours have we ever passed so pleasantly as, when sitting in a circle, in the front room of a restaurant, or in the barroom of a hotel, listening to the war incidents which they were ever ready to relate.

One man stated that he was behind the stone wall at the fight of Marye's Heights [Fredericksburg, December 13, 1862] and how a soldier of the Mass. 19th fell close to the wall. The speaker reached over amid the bullets and drew him inside and attempted to staunch the flow of blood from his wounds.

"But," said he, "the poor fellow died before morning, and many was the message he sent by me to his family in Salem, but I hain't found 'em, an' the poor fellow lies in the [National]Cemetery yonder yet."[The soldier may have been Private Alfred A. Raymond, Jr.,of Company H,recorded as missing in action.]

Others told in a joking way how they used to make little boats and fill them with tobacco, trimming the little sails and sending them across the river to the "Yanks" to come back shortly filled with sugar. One stated that he found one day, on the field in the pocket of a dead soldier, the very plug of tobacco he had exchanged the day before. Many and loud were the praises loaded upon the Massachusetts troops,when those Virginians learned we were from Massachusetts. One said he never saw such "consarned devils" for fighting as there were in the 1st, 10th, 13th, and 38th Massachusetts [the 38th during 1864],and the speaker stated with emphasis, that they "reconed sometimes that those Yanks hated us like pisen." We might have stated from experience that the relator was partially correct, but we consented for the sake of harmony to hold our peace.Hundreds of incidents they related of prisoners they had met, of wounded men they had cared for or been obliged to leave in agony, by the command of their officers.

RICHMOND

A far different state of things exists in Richmond from that which we found at Fredericksburg. Here on every side are the indications of thrift and enterprise. The immense water power of the James at this point is fast being improved by Yankee ingenuity and industry;mills and factories in full operation speak of prosperity and bode good to the once fated city. Belle Isle [in the James River]is stirring with manufactories.Castle Thunder [former Confederate prison]is filled with tobacco, while every store room in Libby [Confederate] Prison is crowded with merchandise. Where Union prisoners expired in agonies of starvation the merchant now has his counting-room; the trades-man, his tons of produce; or the manufacturer, his buzzing machinery. Crowded with visitors from the North seeking for a good investment for capital, the city has a grand prospect of prosperity before it, and already lays claim to the rather premature title of "Second Lowell" [Massachusetts city then famous as a textile manufacturing center; known as the "City of Spindles."].

Richmond is a strange city now. Gorgeous marble buildings have risen, phoenix-like, from the ashes of their predecessors, and around them stand the staggering, ghastly ruins of warehouses and mills destroyed at the [Confederate] evacuation [April 2-3, 1865]. Blackened and shattered walls have, in many instances, received a new roof. Buildings partially burned have been reconstructed and, like their original owners, present a queer combination of the good and bad, the old and the new.

The Tredegar Iron [Works] mills, so celebrated for their surpassing workmanship displayed in the manufacture of cannons, [torpedoes (that is, mines), submarines, and iron plates] now occupy a building on their old site [on the canal], surrounded by an acre of tall ruins. [Tredegar was the chief ordnance factory of the South.] The Gallego [Flour] Mills have recently constructed a large five-story structure on the ground formerly occupied by them near the canal. When the rebels left the city they set fire to the stores along one side of Main Street, and the warehouses, for half a mile, were destroyed. But the restless, speculating Yankee has rebuilt the whole street, and beautiful warehouses of stone and brick now ornament this part of the burned district.

The State House, occupied during the rebellion as the capitol of the Confederacy, is in an exceedingly dilapidated condition. The seats of senators and representatives are rickety and broken; the desks are covered with uncouth figures, initials and wry lettering carved by the ruthless hands of soldiers. Nothing but the old chair in which sat Jefferson and Washington has been respected. The walls are daubed, the doors and stairways are worn and decaying, while the exterior of the building is cracked and scarred by the action of frost in the cleaving mastic.

In the Mayor's office on the second floor we witnessed the "trial" of provisional Governor [Henry Horatio] Wells [a Union army officer who had been a Richmond lawyer four years] for [allegedly] opening a letter addressed to another person. It was an amusing "trial"—all gab and very little law. That the charges were trumped up by the old secessionists of Virginia to affect Governor Wells's political prospects [as a Republican candidate for governor that year] there cannot be a doubt. Everybody regarded it in that light. The courtroom was crowded with all the politicians of the land, and many tough rebellious speeches were made. We feared the unstable old building would fall when the "counsel for the prosecution" flew in a rage, stamped his feet and clapped his hands, declaiming against the oppressors of "Old Virginia."

We could not avoid the mental admission that he was right when he said that Virginia was "ruled by the stranger." [Wells had been a colonel in a Michigan infantry regiment.] For every office, from governor to justice of the peace, seems to be appropriated by Northern men. Under the military rule the soldiers who remained here at the close of the war have been appointed to office, and one would think Boston had depopulated itself in filling the vacant official positions of this State. The mayors, judges, magistrates, sheriffs, inspectors, revenue collectors, post officers, road surveyors, detectives and police, nearly all came from the North, and it seems to be no exaggeration to say that every alternate one comes from Boston.

The original office-holders walk the streets with their hands in their pockets—where they now keep their anger and chivalry—and occupy their time in gazing on the rising monuments of Yankee enterprise, or dream away their hours in the "Academy" [theater on Broad Street?] listlessly watching the mazes of the French can-can. Such being the state of things, we do not wonder that the remaining Virginia lawyers who are allowed to practice should once in a while taunt their rulers with oppression.

Belle Isle is a place of but little interest at present to any one except those who were held there as prisoners of war. It is simply a little hill set down in the middle of the James River at the Rapids. The nail works on one side, which were in full blast during the war, emit the same stream of black smoke to-day. The camping ground on the flat at the foot of the hill, where Union soldiers dragged out a miserable existence, is now ploughed up and used as a garden. The foundations of the old soup house and the graves of the dead still remain—the former to revive again that mockery of feeding the captives, and the latter to remind one of the simple and harsh burial service succeeding the death of comrades. The little old church in which divine service was conducted, and to which the unfortunate soldiers had access, has become a dwelling house, and so completely remodeled as to disguise its former character.

Along the beach where trod the rebel guards, the workmen in the nail factory now draw up their canoes. The old sycamore, near which lay the path to the river, and against which the guard so often leaned to rest, has become a mooring post for skiffs and [other] boats. The fish traps in the broad stream that so often were blocked with the bodies of soldiers who were shot or drowned while attempting to cross the river still stand as a source of revenue to the poor whites on the opposite bank. A flower bed now blooms in the place where stood the rickety hospital tent in which so many soldiers lay suffering and dying—lingering in misery there rather than go to certain death at the Chimborazo Hospital [in Richmond]. How many a man has lain there through the feverish night, listening to the ceaseless roar of the cataracts around him and gazing at the red glare on the canvas reflected from the chimneys of the Tredegar Iron Works, thinking of food on his own table he was never to taste and of a dear mother or wife he was never to see!

Here [as prisoners of war in 1864] died Sergeant [Henry C.] French and [Private] Arthur Dunn of the Mass. 39th, Sergeant [Charles H.] Boswell of the 36th, and [Private] George H. Nichols of the 32nd, whose history we have heard repeated to-day. The graveyard, where the dead were buried just outside the camp, was so near the river that since the removal of bodies to the cemetery, at least one half of it has washed away.

When we were conversing with acquaintances, since
our visit to Belle Isle, in regard to the suffering there, a [former] Confederate soldier came up
and exhibited a beautiful gold watch bearing the
inscription, "To E.D.M., from Maria," which he said
a friend of his bought off a prisoner for five loaves
of bread. Since then we have seen coats, pen-knives,
rings, &c, which were exchanged by Union soldiers for
a single meal.

Libby Prison has not changed materially in its
outward look, having the same dingy appearance. Inside, however, it has undergone great changes. Par-
titions have been built, doorways walled up, cells
for close confinement torn out, and each apartment
fitted up for the uses for which it was built [or-
iginally the warehouse of Thomas Libby & Son, Ship
Chandlers and Grocers]. The cellars are filled with
bales of cornstalks and boxes of merchandise, while
the upper stories are filled with all the variety
of goods found in any commission warehouse. In one
a man is employed as a clerk who was a prisoner
there for over a year. In tearing down the walls
little notes to friends, keepsakes, &c, were found
stowed away, to be recovered if the prisoners ever
returned. Nearly all of these have been destroyed
or sent away to the friends to whom they were addressed.

The balcony around Castle Thunder [Confederate
prison], on which trod the sentinels, has been torn
down. The outside has been painted crimson and the
inside renovated and changed. It is now used as a
tobacco manufactory, and over a hundred hands are
employed drying, pressing, and rolling tobacco. It
is surrounded by ruins, and it is a matter of surprise that, in the great conflagration when the city
was destroyed, Libby and Castle Thunder should be
omitted.

PETERSBURG

Yesterday and today! Petersburg March 8th, 1865
[Conwell's wedding day; hence he was not then in
Petersburg.] and Petersburg, March 8th, 1869.
Then and now! The shrieking crash of guns in Fort
Stedman, the perpetual roar of distant batteries,
and the constant rattle, rattle, rattle of musket-

ry from the long picket line. It was scarcely noticed then, however, so mechanical and business-
like did it seem. Across the narrow ravine our
pickets lay levelling their deadly pieces at the
loop-holes a few feet in front, from which protrud-
ed the muzzles of rebel muskets. No showing of
their heads then. No looking over the breastworks;
for such rashness always drew certain death from
the rifles of the wary foe.

Men were brought back through the covered way and
laid on stretchers to die or to be taken to the
rear.behind the line of earthworks connecting our
posts, from the Appomattox [River] to "Fort Hell"
[Fort Sedgwick], lay the fatigued, emaciated veterans of a hundred battles, one-half of whom were
destined never to hear the cry of victory. Long,
dark lines of Union soldiers lay in the woods in
the rear, and the shouts of sergeants for details
or the commands of division officers could be heard
at every lull in the storm of iron. Overhead, at
frequent intervals, hissed a shot or shrieked a
shell, and men turned carelessly to look and note
where it struck as it crashed through the trees.
Death was as familiar as our rations of hard tack.

"John has been peppered," "Charley has got his
last shot," or "David has gone under" were frequent
remarks as some poor soldier was taken to the rear.
Whenever an orderly would pass from "Fort Hell" the
cry would arise, "How's the fight?" And almost in-
variably the answer was, "Hot as Damnation," and on
he went to the Appomattox. But not withstanding
the shot and the thunder, the day was unusually
quiet. A day of rumors rather than events.

The news came once or twice that the 1st, 2nd, 15th,
19th, and 20th Massachusetts, with the Connecticut
regiments, were "gobbled up." That was no sooner
replaced with a tale of their heavy losses than information came that orders had been issued by Gen.
Grant for the 9th and 6th corps to charge on "Fort
Damnation" [a Confederate fort]. A few moments after
news of Sherman's victorious march and Sheridan's
wonderful raid seemed to fill every soldier's mouth
at the same instant. Later in the day a member of
General Grant's staff rode down the line. "No cheering, boys!" exclaimed the officers of the day as
the boys arose to hurrah for the aide of their be-

loved chieftain. Hard life. Living in holes six
feet underground; and dull even amidst the constant
booming of cannon and the often-repeated observations, "Three more killed at Fort Morton," or "Two
wounded in front of Fort Haskell."
What sights and sounds rush again upon our imagination! Smoke-besmeared faces of New York artillerymen—torn uniforms, bandaged heads and arms—
the piles of sand bags and rows of spades—reliefs
filing in and out of the forts—the forest behind
the work filled with constantly shifting bodies of
infantry—the long line of breastworks of the enemy
nearly parallel with ours—the drooping flags of
both armies—the glitter of bright cannons—the
laughter and the groans—the smiles and the sighs
—the clattering drums and the roll calls—new
graves when the comrades fell—the tin plates and
the empty haversacks—[observation] balloons and
signal flags.

March 8th, 1869 has come, and the traveller finds
many of the fortifications [around Petersburg] entire. But the cannon and the musketry have ceased
their thunders, and the "brave boys . . . are gone."
[From Henry C. Work's Civil War song "Brave Boys
Are They."] The farmer's plough now breaks the soil
where bivouacked the Second Corps, and the great
plantation extends along the southern side of the
Federal lines from "Fort Hell" to Hatcher's Run.
The Negroes, who as slaves threw up the rebel works,
now as freemen dig them down again in search for
old lead. The "Crater" under which [in July 1864]
delved the [48th] Pennsylvanians [from Fort Morton]
to blow to the sky the fort [Elliott's Salient]
and its Carolinian defenders [outside Petersburg]
has now become a "show" and twenty-five cents
apiece is charged to those who visit it. [For a
veteran's narrative of the Battle of the Crater
(which he calls the "battle of the mine") see "Captured by Rebels: A Vermonter at Petersburg, 1864,"
Vermont History (Autumn 1968), p. 231-232.]

The chevaux-de-frise [obstacle of wooden spikes]
by which Forts Davis and Sedgwick ["Fort Hell"]
were surrounded has now become the insurmountable
fence of a peaceful Negro farmer. The covered way
from Fort Stedman to the [Petersburg & City Point]
railroad has caved in, and the dam in the creek,

built at such an expense of life, has now become
almost obliterated. The magazines and bomb-proofs
in Forts Stedman and Washburne [probably Wadsworth, as shown on official military maps.] remain
as uninviting as ever. The huge shell, having done
its errand of death, is now used for the corner-
stone of children's play-houses. The bullets, once
aimed at the hearts of men, and left imbedded in
the earth, are now sold by the Negroes at $100 per
ton. The logs that our boys tugged to the front,
for an abutment in the earthworks, are now being
used for kindling wood in the fashionable residences of Petersburg. The shot and shell are fast
being melted into ploughshares and machinery and
the missiles of war become the instruments of peace.
Southern agriculturists now cut the corn and barley
in the same forts where four years ago the sickle
of Death reaped a rich harvest of human bodies.

The old stump behind which so many of the 29th
and 57th Massachusetts sheltered themselves from
time to time has become the corner of a Negro hut.
The spot where [Confederate] General [Cadmus M.]
Wilcox pitched his tent is to be occupied by a
coal pit.

The old Blandford Church [built about 1735] on
the hill [Crater Road] looks as battered, forsak-
en, and dismal as ever, while the little white
cross in front of it, bearing the inscription,
"Our Dead," is all that marks the resting place of
several thousand Confederate dead. In the shattered
and dry tree tops, along Hatcher's Run, the robins
and the blue birds sing. The scorched timbers of
Poplar Grove Church [The church, whose ruins Conwell saw in 1869, was erected by the New Yorkers,
largely of pine logs.] remind us forcibly of the
famous "New York Carpenters" [nickname of the 50th
Regiment, New York Engineers, skilled and rapid
bridge builders]. But the graves of our comrades
which dotted the fields in every direction when
[Confederate] Fort Gregg was taken and Petersburg
surrendered [April 2, 1865] are now gone. The kind
hands of comrades have removed the sleepers from
their ill-made graves and picked up the bones of
the neglected ones, who, without a grave or a funeral rite, lay in the leaves or grass when our
troops moved on. [The National Cemetery was es-

tablished on the site of the Poplar Grove Church in 1866 and has 6,186 interments of which nearly 4,000 are unknown.]

But the resting places of all are not yet found, and on the day of your correspondent's visit, two bodies were turned up by the ploughshare of the farmer near Fort Stedman,with which were found the rusty metalic letters,M-A-S-S,and a figure 2. All such are carefully buried in the neat cemetery which stands between the Weldon Railroad and Hatcher's Run, on our line of works, and a great satisfaction it is to know that our brothers,although their headboards may be marked "Unknown," are nevertheless in a beautiful cemetery,with a mound of roses blooming above their heads.

It has fallen to the lot of your correspondent to survey [two years ago] the battlefields of Blenheim,Austerlitz,Selferino, and Sadowa [in Europe] and we have been told by guides that on each was decided the fate of the world. But what were they, with their few thousand men and deaths that are enumerated among the hundreds, to the hundreds of thousands of veterans and tens of thousands of dead which make sadly interesting the battlefields of Petersburg! How strange, too, that while hundreds of Americans visit the battlefield of Waterloo weekly, only now and then one takes the pains to visit this field, in his own land, where at least one of the world's greatest battles was fought!

COLD HARBOR

How sleep the brave who sink to rest
By all their country's wishes blest!
[William Collins, "Ode."]

A Prussian officer, accompanied by a colonel of a British regiment, who was surveying the Battlefield of Cold Harbor [northeast of Richmond] just before our visit, is said to have accused the keeper of the cemetery at that point of telling a falsehood, for saying that the Union line of works was fourteen miles long. But when they rode along the fortifications and had been on the road for two hours, they began to believe the cemetery keeper's story, and constantly exclaimed, "Begar,bon coontree!" "wonderful! astonishing!" etc. And even

to an American who knows full well the strength of
our army, the magnitude of this battle is seldom
comprehended. Many a soldier—and even Grant himself—has returned to the field since the war and
could not find one familiar spot. So great is the
change from a field of armies to a barren plain.
The battle-field of Cold Harbor has been of especial concern to us as there fell so many of our
friends and acquaintances [in the Wilderness Campaign in 1864]. It was with feelings of the deepest interest we tramped about through pine groves,
over sandy fields,ravines and breastworks,follow-
ing in the footsteps of the men we knew. Long we
lingered about the angles occupied by the 10th,
27th, 25th, 19th, 11th, and 12th Massachusetts and
searched about as if some memento might be left to
tell where our friends stood in that terrible hour.
Two thousand killed in ten minutes! [The Union
Army lost 7,000 men in a few hours.]No other battle of the war has such a history as that.Ah,that
was a terrible day! [Some writers have called it
the most horrible slaughter of the entire Civil
War.]
And as we thought it over, we sat down upon the
earth-works which the 25th Massachusetts and 7th
Connecticut threw up with their tin cups and plates,
and then we counted over the troops from our native
State who participated in that fight [June 1-12,
1864].The 7th, 21st, 20th, 9th, 11th, 12th, 13th,
15th, 16th, 18th, 19th, 58th, 59th, 35th, 28th, 32d,
40th, 37th, 27th, 25th Infantry, 1st [Regiment]
Heavy Artillery, the 1st, 5th, 9th, 10th, 11th, 14th
Light [Artillery] Batteries were there, and consequently this field must be of especial interest
to Massachusetts men; and there, too, were the 2d,
5th, and 6th New Hampshire, the 7th and 11th Connecticut—but why enumerate? For hardly a State or
town in the North that did not lose a valuable citizen in the first ten minutes of the fight [there
around New Cold Harbor] on the morning of June 3,
1864 [in the closing phase of General Grant's Wilderness Campaign].
Our province is not with the history of the field
but with its present condition. The **earth-works**
are fast disappearing under the hands of the dili-
gent lead searchers,who are found everywhere along

the line. A profitable business they make of it,
too. Tons of old iron and lead are carted into
Richmond from this field, for which a round price
is paid. We met several Negroes, with large sacks,
collecting the bones of dead horses which they sold
to the bone-grinders in Richmond. The trees and
stumps everywhere show the marks of battle, and the
traces of ricocheting shot can be distinctly observed. Much of the field has been ploughed up and
cultivated since the battle, thus destroying many
landmarks that might otherwise be found. But the
ruins of the old Gaines's Mill stand   [on Powhite
Creek] just as they have stood since [General George
B.] McClellan's battle in [June] '62 [in the   Seven
Days Battles near Old Cold Harbor].

But the saddest part of our letter remains. Skeletons and ghosts haunt us in our dreams, and grinning skulls are all we can think of by day. It has
been supposed that the Union dead were all buried
in the cemeteries by the government and that all the
respect due the dead was now shown. But far is this
from the case. The burial corps established a cemetery at Cold Harbor, and took up all the bodies
they could find, and gave them a decent burial, although in one case they were obliged to bury 631
in a single grave, and in another over 300. The
men were then discharged, and no authority [was]
given the cemetery people to proceed any further
with the work. Since then the Negroes have dug up
many bodies, and the bones of Union and Confederate soldiers. We found in all parts of the field
that skulls, ribs, legs, and arm-bones lay scattered about in fearful array, while the bones of
many a poor soldier lay partially exposed through
the action of the rain.

While we were walking along the works we found a
Negro who had just exhumed a body that was buried
in a salient, on the Barker's Mill road, occupied
during the battle by the First [Regiment] Massachusetts [Heavy] Artillery. The clothing and cap
were those of an artilleryman, and a hole in the
skull indicated that he was shot through the head.
With it was found a silver watch, which we purchased
of the Negro and send with this letter to Mr. [Ro-
land] Worthington, proprietor of the *Traveller*, hoping it may be identified. Many a watch has thus

been found, which the Negroes keep or sell. Another body was discovered by a Negro the same day, wrapped in a rubber blanket,bearing the mark,"Co. E,106th N.Y.S.V." [St. Lawrence County Regiment]. The cemetery keeper stated that he had made a report in regard to the bodies, and doubtless the government would soon see them properly buried. [Cold Harbor National Cemtery has 1,958 interments, 1,286 classified unknown.]

SEVEN PINES

[One may easily imagine that] two hundred years ago or more, a party of hunters from Jamestown encamped among the bushes, about six miles from the present site of Richmond,and during the night they were invited to a "corn dance," where their Indian neighbors celebrated the return of harvest. To guard against the danger of losing their way while returning without their dusky guide,they searched for landmarks,and among other things they selected seven pines which grew from the same stump. Chipping these trees with their hatchets,they concluded they could safely return if they should retrace their steps by the "seven pines." Thus was named the spot which, after the lapse of two centuries, was to be known throughout the civilized world as the Battle-field of Seven Pines[and Fair Oaks].

The "seven pines" have decayed long since and their exact location is lost to the present generation,but the forest has doubtless the same primitive appearance today that it had two hundred years ago. If the visitor wanders but a short distance from the muddy highway (unless he fortifies himself against deception)he will surely lose his way. The same dreary, wild, old pines, the same impassable swamps seem to surround him on every side,and if while floundering about in the mud he chance to find the road he may well be thankful for deliverance. Yet here it was, in this mud, around these stench pools, beside these filthy streams, that a gallant [Union] army lay for a month before [Richmond] the almost undefended capital of their foe. They had conquered their enemy, but, like the custom in pugilistic encounters,McClellan was wait-

ing for Jeff Davis to "call time." How aggravating the thought as we tread again the dismal forest
and look upon the falling fortifications and splin-
tered trees to think that when the sun set that
dread first of June [1862], we [the Union army]
could have marched to Richmond and saved 200,000
valuable lives!

> For of all sad words of tongue or pen,
> The saddest are these: "It might have been!"
> [John Greenleaf Whittier, "Maude Muller."]

Nearly all the traces which the army of McClellan left behind,like the fruits of his victories,
have long since passed into oblivion. Here and
there a shattered tree along the line of [General
Silas] Casey's fight, and slight lines of earthworks left by [Brigadier General Edwin V.]Sumner's
and [General Joseph] Hooker's corps are all that
remind one of the [Confederate] storm which burst
upon the Army of the Potomac, May 31, 1862. The
rough rifle pits, and log [bomb] proofs, the old
huts at Savage's Station, the "deadly fence" on
Gaines's farm,the army roads with slough holes and
ruts have entirely disappeared. Some little trace
is still left,however,of the Grape-vine Bridge so
skillfully constructed[over the Chickahominy River from May 28 to 30, 1863] by the 5th [Regiment]
New Hampshire [Infantry] and so nearly destroyed
at the retreat; while by close inspection the bullet holes in the trees, among which the 7th Michigan and 20th Massachusetts [infantry regiments]
made their charge upon the flanking rebel troops,
can still be seen, telling the direction in which
the enemy lay.A wild pine swamp or a desolate wilderness is the best description that can be given
of the field [which is also called Fair Oaks].
A short distance to the south from the bunch of
trees where Casey established his headquarters before the fight is now located the [Seven Pines]Na-
tional Cemetery [with only 150 of its 1,370 dead
"known"]. Its superintendent, [James Kelly, first
official superintendent, who started duty thereOcto-
ber 24, 1868],a jolly soldier from a New York regiment, lives alone in a little house [A wooden
frame structure replaced in 1874 by a brick one

which still stands.], his only companions being the graves of his comrades. War is his life and pride. He lives in the past, and in most graphic manner describes how his regiment [on June 27, 1862] charged over the hills at Gaines's Mill [near Richmond]. With his fingers he enumerates the regiments from the visitor's State, and can tell many a tale of individual prowess that has never been recorded. Of the Tenth and Seventh Massachusetts [both of which fought at Fair Oaks-Seven Pines], he spoke with glowing pride, but there his acquaintance with Massachusetts troops ended. Wounded, worn, and old, having little and caring for less, he spends his days in setting out trees in the cemetery, planting flowers on the graves, or talking with visitors from the time he runs up the flag in the morning until he pulls it down at night.

Close by his door, and beside the long rows of the [1,220] unknown dead, was posted a large white board on which was painted in black letters the following lines [Source unidentified; possibly written by the superintendent or some other Northerner. Board not there now.]:

What heroes braved the battle's crash,
The cannon's roar, the blinding flash,
Here sleep 'neath these lonely mounds of clay,
Unknown to the weeping ones away.
Unknown in this world of joy or pain;
Unknown to the friends that seek in vain;
Unknown till that bright judgment day,
When all friends meet in the faraway.

The day when we, your correspondent, visited Fair Oaks, Savage's Station, Seven Pines, &c., where the Seven Days' Fight began, we were nearly shaking ourself to pieces, humoring the fever and ague, and we shook as if the dread monster was angry at the departure of the army of his victims and was determined to vent his whole spite on us. The rain also poured down in torrents, and thus we were deprived of the usual opportunities of searching for interesting localities and incidents. We wandered about in the White Oak Swamp, and from there [eastward] to the Chickahominy without meeting man or beast. And, had we met one, he must have regarded us as an animated mound of mud.

MALVERN HILL

It is no wonder that Lafayette, in the days of the Revolution [in 1780], selected Malvern Hill [near Richmond] as his headquarters because of the "unexampled beauty of its location." Without a doubt the battle-field is one of the most beautiful spots in Virginia. At the time your correspondent visited the place the green acres of wheat were waving before the wind. The buds were appearing on the trees, the apricots, cherries, and peaches were in full bloom, and birds of brilliant plumage sang delightful songs of spring from every branch. Far away the James River glittered in the sun, disturbed at intervals by the wheels of steamers. How strange to think that these high bluffs were the scene of such a conflict but seven years ago!

The sabres, the bayonets, the muskets, and the cannon are gone and have left no sign. In the deep ravine where thousands fell—where crushing cannon and mutilating cavalry rode roughly over a pavement of human bodies—the little brook laughs on toward the valley, clear and undisturbed as though there never had been war. In the line of woods where the groans of the wounded and the yells of [General] Hooker's Division made wild echo that fatal evening [July 1-2, 1862], to-day the twitter of the robin, the blue bird, the mocking bird, and thrush drive from the mind all thoughts of war. They show us the spot where four hundred dead Confederates were found piled together in their charge on Sedgwick's line. But now a beautiful spring bubbles out of the sand, and brilliant Mayflowers grow there. War? There are no indications of war. Everything is peace. The forest, which was so scarred and battered, between the hill and Willis' [Methodist] Church, has been cut down, and rich grain speaks of prosperity and peace.

Even at Glendale [also called Frayser's Farm, twelve miles southeast of Richmond] a little circular cemetery is all that is left to convince the visitor that death and destruction vied with each other here seven years ago [on June 30, 1862].

Standing at the brick cottage which was McClellan's headquarters on the crest of the hill, and

looking back over the basin-shaped battle-field,we
could not but mark the strong resemblance between
the appearance of this field and that on which [in
1792] was fought the Battle of Valmy, in France.
[In that battle of the French Revolutionary Wars
the invading Austrian-Prussian forces were defeated by the French.] The position of [General Darius
N.] Couch in this battle and that of [General Charles
F.] Dumouriez in the Battle of Valmy were almost
the same in every feature; while Hooker and Sedgwick held a ravine and knoll exceedingly like those
held by Prince Charles [William Ferdinand,Duke of
Brunswick] and [General Francois Christophe de]
Kellermann near the heights of La Lune.

Lee's army,like that of the [Austrian-Prussian]
Allies, lay on two sides of the enemy's position,
and was the assailing party.But when we have marked
the striking similarity between the fields and positions, we can pursue the comparison no farther.
For there is a ridiculous difference between the
action of Kellermann and McClellan. One fought
amidst his troops and by his individual bravery
saved the day;the other spent his time during the
battle whistling on a gunboat,and declared after-
wards that he "knew nothing of the matter." When
[in the summer of 1867]we returned to Chalons[sur-
Marne] from the heights of La Lune we felt proud
for the brave Frenchman. Today, as we turned from
the field of Malvern Hill, we felt ashamed for
McClellan.

When we left Malvern Hill we thought to have
reached New Market Heights [Chapin's Farm] in the
course of an hour,as they were said to be but five
miles away. At this point was made that furious
charge of the colored troops, in the Tenth [Army]
Corps [Army of the James], under General [D. B.]
Birney, while Grant was before Petersburg. Our
road lay through thick clumps of wood,across acres
of fallen timber,and through swollen streams, and
long before a fortification came in sight we had
lost our way. For hours we wandered about, taking
first this road and then that,seeing no habitation
nor a living thing.We had nearly come to the conclusion that we were irretrievably lost, when a
large brick house appeared in the distance,which,
on reaching,we found to belong to Mr. [A. M.] Aik-

en, the proprietor of Aiken's Landing, where [General E.O.C. Ord's] 18th [Army] Corps crossed [the James River] from Bermuda Hundred to attack Fort Harrison.

Here a young lady offered to guide us to the Heights, and then to Dutch Gap. We say a young lady! But she would hardly be called a lady in the North, we think. If a young lady can have dirty hands, poor teeth, dozy eyes, towsley red hair, and wear an old homespun, ragged dress, and have a form which indicated the entire absence of bustles, hoops, paper collars, cotton, and paint —and have her toes out—and then can squat in the bottom of an old two-wheeled mule cart, with which the farm work is done, and with one rein drive a mule, jolting through deep creeks, over logs, along steep embankments, with entire resignation—then, perhaps, we are right in calling our guide a young lady. Yet she was the daughter of one of Virginia's proudest sons who owns 1500 acres of beautiful land and at whose house a feast was preparing for the fox hunters. Yet she, or the mule, knew the way well, and soon New Market Heights were pointed out to us.

NEW MARKET HEIGHTS

The lines of fortifications, as far as we could see along the high ground, were defended in front by a half-mile of fallen timber through which it seemed to us to be utterly impossible for a man to make his way, much less make a successful charge. Yet, through the marshes, across the streams, climbing over logs and through brush, the brave black men [who included the Connecticut 29th Infantry] charged successfully on this important position, September 29th, 1864. No white regiments ever made a bolder or more skillful charge. The works all stand entire as the army left them at the evacuation of Richmond, except here and there a magazine which has borne down its decaying timbers. The capture of this place by General Butler's command was one of the most important movements of the campaign around Petersburg.

DUTCH GAP CANAL

The next point of interest was Dutch Gap Canal, where General Butler attempted to shorten the James River seven miles, as it makes almost a circle in its windings through the valley.here we found the canal in a good condition, and it would be navigable but for the fact that the owner of the island has filled up a place in it wide enough for a road in order to have communication with[both parts of] his land.General Butler here shrewdly put Confederate prisoners at work to quiet the rebel battery that shelled the canal from the Howlett House [across the river].But the Howlett House is now in ruins, the canal is useless,the rebels are silenced, and General Butler is in Congress [as a representative from Massachusetts]. And here let us remark how amusingly the people conduct themselves in regard to Ben Butler.In several places we have seen children whose fathers are bringing them up to hate Butler,and we have heard the following catechism pass between father and child:

"John, who do you love best?"
"Bob Lee."
"Who do you hate the mightiest?"
"Ben Butler."
"Good boy. Go and get some cake."

FORT HARRISON

From Dutch Gap we proceeded at once to Fort Harrison which is an earthwork of considerable strength, about three miles from the canal. Here was made another terrible charge by colored troops from the Tenth Corps,under direction of General Butler, on the same day that New Market Heights were captured. Here, too, the Confederates made three tremendous charges to retake it,being each time repulsed with a loss of whole brigades. The fort is almost entire, and a colored farmer now occupies the only remaining hut within it as a dwelling house.

Here is one of the neatest and best arranged National cemeteries we have seen, in which colored and white troops [totaling 817] who fell in this vicinity are buried side by side.All honor to the men, be they white or black,that would charge two

miles over a level plain of fallen trees,and then
up a steep hill and over a deep ditch,to dislodge
the foe. Let them sleep in peace. The cemetery
keeper offered to act as our guide, and after showing us the fort and its adjacent lines of rifle-
pits, he escorted us to a large field on the north-
west side of the fort, and there a most terrible
scene presented itself. The thousands of Confederate soldiers, who had fallen in their desperate
and persistent attempts to retake Fort Harrison,
had been buried by the Confederates where they fell.
Twenty acres or more have just been ploughed up
by the owner of the field and the ploughshare turned
to the surface all these skeletons.Over the whole
tract the bones are strewed in profusion,and grinning skulls stare the visitor in the face on every
hand. When the farmer was questioned, he said the
land was now the richest piece he had,and in jus-
tification of his sacrilegious act stated that he
"didn't put 'em there nohow." We learned after-
wards that [some of] the bones had been taken away
by the cart-load and sold to fertilizing mills in
Richmond. Two humane men, too poor to do anything
else, came the day we were there and attempted to
burn some of the bones to prevent some of the wretch-
es from carting them off.But a long job they will
have if they attempt to burn them all.
Yet these are not the only fields of Confederate
bones we have seen, nor the first instance of dis-
respect for their dead we have witnessed. Perhaps
they are too poor, as they plead, to bury them.
Then, in the name of humanity, why do they rear a
stone monument,forty-five feet square at the base
and ninety feet high,at Richmond to the memory of
the "Confederate dead" in the cemetery, and leave
their bones to bleach and crumble on the fields?
Strange people, these Virginians. Their ways are
inexplicable to us.

FORT DARLING

The last trip we made before taking our final
leave of Richmond gave us a better idea of the engineering skill displayed by the rebel army than
we ever had before.We left Richmond at nine o'clock
in the morning, and, crossing the [James] river,

wandered about all day in the vicinity of Fort Darling and Bermuda Hundred. Fort Darling is one of
the most skillfully constructed works we ever saw,
and after four years the earthworks remain entire.
Situated on a high bluff [Drewry's Bluff] some
seventy feet above the river [five miles south of
Richmond], and at one of the sharp bends of that
meandering stream, its guns could sweep the river
lengthwise for miles. The earthworks themselves are
twelve feet high and nearly fifteen feet through.
Underground passageways connect each salient of the
fort with the others and with the adjoining rifle
pits in the fields beyond. A ditch twenty feet
deep, and commanded by an enfilading battery, ran
along the front of the works, beyond which was an
almost impregnable abattis [obstacle of felled
trees]. The magazines were covered with thirty
feet of earth, and everything was built in a most
substantial manner.

Here it was that Commodore [John] Rodgers met with
his repulse when attempting to aid McClellan in the
[unsuccessful] capture of Richmond in 1862. It
would seem that these heavy, hundred-pound guns [at
the fort] would annihilate anything that could float
in the river. The monitors [such as Rodgers's
Weehawken] might have run by this battery had it not
been for the obstructions which the rebels placed
in the river, and which are there still. [Rodgers
also commanded the vessel, *Galena,* in the bombardment of Fort Darling in 1862.] The sunken iron
vessels turned the current of the river, and after
washing away two acres of the opposite bank, the
stream has made a channel for itself beyond the
sunken vessels and opposite Fort Darling. At the
time of our visit a large number of workmen with
tugs and flat boats were endeavoring to raise the
old hulks, and the iron deck of one was just appearing above the water. They expect an appropri-
ation from Congress to enable them to clear the
channel, although the present enterprise seems to
be simply for the sake of the vessels, if sound,
and for the iron, if not.

BERMUDA HUNDRED

The lines at Bermuda Hundred are fast disappearing before the rain storms, and in another year they will begin to lose their identity. They were evidently very strong, especially the Federal line which extends across the peninsula from river to river. The appearance of the spot is much changed. The old barracks are torn down and the fields are covered with waving wheat. The town of Bermuda Hundred [settled in 1616 as a Jamestown Settlement colony], down near the landing, is now nothing but a collection of rude, white-washed Negro huts built around a still worse hovel in which an F.F.V. ["First Family of Virginia"] keeps a "store." There he now sells gingham and molasses, jewsharps and kerosene oil, together with such pieces of ham and beef as he can get by trade of the farmers. The sea of white tents, with their gay flags, uniforms, and stirring music, is gone. No gunboats stand in the river. No sound of war on shore. No trade in shad among the soldiers now. No one to raid the melon or cucumber patches. Those lively days are gone with the Yankees. The old days have returned. All is quiet.

CITY POINT

From Bermuda Hundred we rowed across the James to City Point [later to become a part of Hopewell], a place of considerable note [and a base of operations] during Grant's campaign [in 1864-65 against Petersburg]. But it is a shabby place now. Only one old wharf for the steamers to make a landing and no warehouse of any kind. The old houses upon the hill stand as they did during the Petersburg campaign; no additions, none destroyed, as we could perceive. The postmaster had the fever and ague, and the cemetery keeper was too lame to be of any assistance. So we "did" City Point in a hurry, being exceedingly glad when we were on the [railroad] cars for Petersburg.

HARRISON'S LANDING

The day we visited Harrison's Landing, the place which McClellan selected as his base of operations [after the Battle of Malvern Hill], it was raining quite hard, just as it used to do when our army lay there and died by thousands [in 1862]. The old mansion stands as dignified as ever and has been somewhat renovated of late. [This restored James River plantation, now called "Berkeley," was the ancestral home of a signer of the Declaration of Independence and two U.S. presidents.] The old wharf is still entire, although showing great signs of decay. The old camping grounds are ploughed up and sowed with grain, and all the barracks, signal stations and "winter pits" are gone. The graveyard, too, sad resting place of thousands who had no ammunition with which to fight disease, has disappeared, and the dead are removed to other cemeteries. We cannot speak further of Harrison's Landing. It is not a pleasant subject for the soldier to think upon. The memory of the terrible disease [scurvy, in the summer of 1862], and of a nation's disgraces we have no desire to revive. Hastily we will turn from unnecessary and necessary suffering to "the dawn of peace" [Walter Kittredge, "Tenting on the Old Camp Ground."].

APPOMATTOX COURT HOUSE

One hundred miles [westward] in the cars on a rough road [of the Petersburg & Lynchburg line] and you have passed from Petersburg to Appomattox Court House. You would almost suppose you had traveled a thousand miles if you were guided in your conclusions by the scenery. For, instead of pine swamps and sandy fields, here is a mountainous country, well stocked with oak and elm, and spotted here and there with the points of dark rocks and ledges. One needs to have been here at the surrender to appreciate the scenery now. The appearance of the fields is more attractive than that of the [tidewater] lowlands of Eastern Virginia. But otherwise there is nothing unusual to attract attention —unless, perchance, the shot holes in the build-

ings about the depot be worth inspection.But this
was not a battle-field; less than 200 men were
killed here. [In the little cemetery nearby are
buried 18 Confederate soldiers and one unknown Union
soldier.] Yet it is one of the most important places
mentioned in modern history. From this spot went
forth [on Palm Sunday, April 9,1865] those potent
words, so full of joy, to make glad the hearts of
500,000 veterans and 20,000,000 people: "Lee has
surrendered!"

Do you remember those words,ye soldiers,who had
been so long wishing for the dawn of peace? Do you
who were so fortunate as to camp upon one of those
hill sides remember how you felt as you looked down
into the valley where Lee and Grant were settling
the terms of surrender? What a scene for an art-
ist! Yet none have done it justice. Perhaps it
could not be painted.

The little clear stream[Appomattox River]in the
valley beside which stands the orchard where Lee
first raised the flag of truce;the two old houses
with their log barns a little behind and above the
orchard; the old,square-roofed Court House on the
hill, with its clump of houses, among which is
[Major Wilmer] McLean's,where [in the parlor] the
terms of surrender were agreed upon; the groves of
green oaks dotting the hillsides for miles around,
filled with recumbent soldiers and lines of gun
stacks; the troops of [General Philip H.] Sheridan's horses grazing in the edge of the woods on
the left;the glittering cannon to the east of the
Court House; the side of the highway, filled with
old Confederate blankets, guns and mule carts;
mud-besmeared staff officers riding furiously up
and down the hills; the smoke of a thousand camp
fires; the steadily moving columns of bluecoated
veterans appearing in the distance, as they come
in from the fields where but two hours before they
had received the glad order, "Cease firing!"; the
waving of tattered flags from the knolls,the trees,
and the house-tops; the flutter of signal flags
and the waving of hats;the long, gray,shabby line
of the enemy with its flags motionless and their
defenders stretched on the earth for rest—combined, with the distant booming of cannon not yet
silenced by the arrival of "new orders";the shouts

of men; the rattle of sabres; the rumbling sounds of approaching artillery and cavalry; the song of the New York Battery as it struck up [George Root's] "Battle Cry of Freedom," mingled with the hoarse orders of brigade and regimental officers, and the ring of bayonets and newly arrived divisions stacking their arms, and a thousand dins we have no time or space to describe—all did their part while engraving the scene on the tablet of every grateful soldier's heart!

How the shouts went up when all was over! Massachusetts veterans were going to their workshops, Maine troops to their lumber yards, Vermont and New Hampshire infantry to their flocks [The Report of the United States Commissioner of Agriculture for 1865 shows the two states had 2,054,867 sheep but only 236,734 cows.], New York raiders to their vineyards and orchards, Western "bummers" to their broad acres, and New Jersey "blues" to the land of Camden and Amboy [The long-popular phrase —used by politicians and railroad promoters — was "the State of Camden and Amboy," referring to the State supported Camden and Amboy Railroad.]—while all were soon to see the fathers, mothers, sisters, wives, daughters, and sons they had left so long. Amply repaid did the soldier feel then for his long marches, poor rations, days of sickness, sleepless nights, shivering days, narrow escapes, and wounds when he saw the country for miles around strewn with the trappings of rebel soldiers and knew that the remnant left would march away disarmed on the morrow, and they—poor [Yankee] "devils"—had at last got their wish and were truly going to "God's country." How many said to the quartermaster that night, "Give us a hard tack and let us go home." But alas! we [the Union Army] didn't go home. The hard tack was given to the 20,000 greybacks and *they* were permitted to go home, while we were kept to parade around Washington!

But Appomattox today looks deserted and sad; no flags; no guns; no soldiers. The tree in the orchard where Lee hoisted his flag of truce has been rooted up for mementoes and its companion is also nearly gone. The old white houses on opposite sides of the Court House settlement look as they did when used as "headquarters."

HAMPTON

We have spent a night in the dirty, one-story town of Hampton [Virginia], where a hamlet of Negroes and "poor whites" has sprung up in place of the wealthy village owned by rich planters before the war, and where now small lager-beer shops and two-penny stores hem the sandy highway, and drunken white man, unruly Negroes, and stray pigs make the day uncomfortable and the night hideous. It was a beautiful town before the war. Its large, vine-covered mansions, ancient churches, and attractive [Chesapeake] Female College buildings, surrounded by thrifty plantations and hedge-bordered gardens, called to the shade of its fig trees the wealthiest men and the most beautiful ladies of the Sunny South.

But [Confederate General John B.] Magruder sent a company of men, in which were many natives of the town [August 7, 1861], with strict orders to burn the town, and well they performed their mission. When the great Army of the Potomac, under [General] McClellan, landed there [early in 1862] nothing but sooty ruins and clouds of ashes remained for them to quarter in. [Only five houses survived the fires.] The noble structure [founded in 1854], formerly the Female College, and then a hospital, stood then, as it remains now, looking proudly down upon the quiet waves of the harbor, surrounded by rubbish and desolation. Many that came with that gallant army and who subsequently lay in the college building (which [during the war] bore the appellation of Chesapeake [Military] Hospital), now lie silent and cold in the [Hampton] National Cemetery near by, above them a towering monument of New England granite and above that the starry flag. [The fund for it was raised by Dorothea Dix, Civil War nurse and social reformer.] From the top of the hospital the [returning] soldier can see the old walls of the dilapidated church, and his old camping place, the parade grounds where he drilled and drilled until he had rather be shot at than don his accoutrements.

FORTRESS MONROE

On the point [Old Point Comfort] stand the dark walls of Fortress Monroe, unchanged in any respect, and out in the harbor the unfinished derrick-covered Rip-Raps [a shoal called Fort Wool], the anchored shipping, and at low tide the black, craggy hull of the submerged *Merrimac* [alias *Virginia*, scuttled May 11, 1862]. From the walls of Fortress Monroe still frowns the big "Union gun" [During the war called the "Lincoln Gun," it had a fifteen-inch bore and weighed twenty-four tons.], surrounded by numerous "dogs of war" [William Shakespeare, *Julius Caesar*.], and the day we stood by it and looked down upon the familiar pavement, the casemates, and the headquarters, where, when we last stood there [as a captain in a Massachusetts regiment in 1863] we saw General Butler pacing the porch [of his command headquarters], we thought again of war, and our companion brought the history of the place vividly to mind by saying:

"Here began the real fight. Here was a man in command who dared tell the slaves that they were free. Here was started [by Benjamin Franklin Butler] the word 'contraband' as applied to men; which in legal phrase meant captured property, but which to the Negro meant liberty, as General Butler well knew."

Ah! thought we, strike General Butler's name and acts out of the history of our late war, and it would seem to have begun with no defined object and been conducted for no purpose. Confederate soldiers say: "If we had killed him we would not have failed," and the rebel traitors and Ku-Klux of to-day hate the very sight of his name. There in Fortress Monroe were laid the plans and given the orders which, if they did not always gain a victory, did at least prevent the success of the rebellion.

A VIRGINIA MARKET WAGON

Ho! Ho! What a cart! What a cow! What a woman! If you could have been there to see them you would have laughed until you had cried. The wheels—and there were only two—had six spokes made of round saplings, just as they came from the forest. The hubs were square blocks of wood with willow strips nailed around them to prevent splitting—the felloes were ash rails bent around the spokes and tied on—the axeltree was an ash tree with the knots sticking out in every direction—the shafts or thills were round undressed poles, and the "box" was a skeleton frame made of rails in which were many useless auger holes, while the whole "keerige" was of the most primitive order.

On a round pole, which was supported by two slender uprights, sat a corpulent woman with a foot on each shaft, a big basket of vegetables suspended at her back from a rope around her waist, and a single rein held firmly in both hands, which prevented the aforesaid basket from pulling her over backward. The strange vehicle and the strange, dirty, sour-faced, bonnetless rider were drawn by a little, chuckleheaded specimen of a cow, which had been kept on a low diet so long that she would have answered well for a skeleton museum. What little hide she had left was really fit for no other purpose but to hold her awkward bones together. The piece of a clothes line which served the purpose of a guide, as well as to preserve the equilibrium of the Amazonian driver, was fastened to the only unbroken horn and was lashed against the side of the cow, to turn, in case the driveress wished, to the right; while a nervous jerk indicated the desire of the mistress that her cowship should "haw," or turn to the left.

Such was the "establishment" and such the driver. But the passenger, who sat uneasily on the bare poles and hung his legs out over the rear end of the cart, whose clothes were covered with mud, whose eyes were sleepy and stomach empty, and who gave an audible sigh as the no-springed vehicle rattled over the stones, was no less a personage than the wandering correspondent of the Boston *Daily Traveller*.

The proprietress had a tongue which rattled, squealed, blubbered, and squeaked, resembling the cart in every respect but one: the cart needed lubrication, her tongue did not. The unpleasant tenor of her conversation, the hard uncertain seat, together with the anxiety lest the weight of your correspondent—which nearly equalled that of the cow—should cause the rear of the cart to go down and the shafts with the cow to come up and over, made the journey from Hampton to Big Bethel uninteresting, unpleasant, ridiculous.

"Couldn't yer sell yer wegetables?" said a mischievous darkey we met, who eyed us sidewise, as much as to say: Everything *green* about your load is not among your vegetables.

"No, siree," said she of the whip and spur, "tew cents fur carits and ninepunce fur aags wont pay their haulin. Shant cum tew Hampton agin, soon."

The darkey showed his ivory, gave a low "eh! eh!" and trudged off, while we lumbered on toward the disastrous field of Big Bethel. The roads improved as we went inland, and we found ourselves at last at Big Bethel. The fat woman thanked us for our money, shoved it under her vegetables, shouted "Gee lang!" hit the cow behind with her foot, and after a splashing, squeaking voyage through the shallow creek, disappeared in the forest. Who knows but that she is as happy and contented in her unstable gocart, on the road to Yorktown, as the silk-dressed, jewel-rigged ladies of Boston are in their carriage-and-four on the road to [the suburb of] Brighton? Thus mused we as we turned from the roadside and clambered upon the still complete fortifications which remind us of war.

Almost the first thing which attracted our attention as we turned into the pine grove beside the stream was a human skull. Half buried in the sand and streaked with black, it seemed to look down toward the rivulet, suggesting the idea that perchance the soldier died on the bank of the stream longing for water. We could only hope that he was not one of the number that was killed [in the Battle of Big Bethel] when our troops, by a blunder, fired into each other. And taking the skull we buried it in the sand beside the stream. In a simple, unostentatious grave, dug out with our hands, with no stone or wood to mark the spot and no prayer or hymn to consign it to rest, lies all that remains of a once brave patriot. The pines will sigh, the birds will twitter, and the stream gurgle on, down through the ages; but their unintelligible requiems will never say to the stranger, "We sigh for the dead" or point out the spot where we laid him.

What cares he? he cannot know.
Lay him low, lay him low.

[Conwell has the lines reversed. They are from George Henry Boker's "Dirge for a Soldier" where, in stanza 1, they appear: "Lay him low,/In the clover or the snow!/What cares he? he cannot know."] After pausing to wonder what home had been made cheerless, what heart had been broken by the fall of the man whose skull we had just buried, we turned away in sadness to look upon the fortifications.

BIG BETHEL

Here and there [at Big Bethel] long mounds covered with little tufts of grass and thickly strewn with pine burrs showed where Magruder fortified himself, and where he displayed his "wonderful sagacity" by running away before a shot had been fired at him or at his command. The signs of the Battle [June 10, 1861], which occurred in a great part between our own troops who [collided with one another when they] disregarded General Butler's instructions and used not the watchword, "Boston," are few, and can be found only by the most observant. But the pang which it gave the public heart cannot soon be forgotten, and the names of Big Bethel and Little Bethel are unpleasant to the Northern ear. [The Union defeat there: Union killed totaled 18; Confederate, only 1]. We found the ruins of two log cabins and the old church, but the cultivation of the land, the growth of underbrush, and the clearing of large tracts have changed the spot greatly since the war. We could tarry but an hour, and while we were sitting on a high mound thinking that we would take a measurement of the works, our expected team came along, and we started at once— this time behind a spirited pony—for Yorktown [about 20 miles north of Hampton].

YORKTOWN

This is a place full of interest, and it was with no little satisfaction that we saw the sun rise clear on the morning after our arrival; for a day is a short time in which to see the war marks of Yorktown, and if you have but one you wish that one to be clear. A soldier who had been in the rebel army kindly offered to escort us about, and a short time convinced us that he was just the man we needed. He hurried us through the shanty-hemmed street to the house ["York Hall"] of [Thomas] Nelson, Jr., who was the first governor [1781] of Virginia and an active agent for the colonies during the American Revolution [and a signer of the Declaration of Independence]. The structure was an old-fashioned three-story brick building occupied by Lord Cornwallis and bombarded by the Americans; but having been recently painted and repaired by a descendant of Nelson, had a neat and comfortable appearance. Its riddled and rickety condition when used by the National troops for quarters and as a hospital would compare very unfavorably with its appearance now.

From this residence we went to "Cornwallis's Cave," where that lord made his headquarters before his surrender [in 1781], and where, during the delay of McClellan [in 1862 during the Peninsular Campaign], Magruder partitioned off a magazine and walled up the entrance. It was a dark cavern, running a hundred feet under the sand bank, near the shore. [The cave, dug out of the marl, is now boarded up, although marked by a road sign.] Near by were some of the strongest lines of earthworks we ever saw, which connected with the circle around the town and inside of which were many dilapidated and partially filled bomb-proofs.

Next, our guide showed us the spot where Lord Cornwallis surrendered to Washington; near which, he stated, was the camp of a Massachusetts regiment [during the Civil War], but as he could remember their fighting better than their number we cannot state which regiment it was. Away hurried our companion as soon as we had glanced at the spot, and anon called our attention to the National Cemetery [with 1,435 unknown dead] where, said he, "Your boys sleep in peace, while ours lie kicking about all over the fields."

When we had seen all there was of interest in the dirty little hamlet called Yorktown, had seen the still ponderous earthworks of the fort near the river, had noted how the guard quarters and provost marshall's offices had been turned into beer shops and livery stables, and how flowers grow in the old graveyard near the ruined church, we left the "city" behind us and rode toward the battle-field. We could hardly call it a battle-field, although huge piles of sand and yawning ditches still remind us of the work which our soldiers did there. For the dam near Wynn's Mill which, with the church and accompanying buildings, is still in ruins, was the only place where fight was offered, and this, except for a daring charge on the part of the Vermonters'[Infantry Regiments 3,4,5, and 6],was only a skirmish in its results. All along the lines, over the ditches, into the woods, around high fortifications, under shell-splintered trees, we rode, scarcely believing it possible that an army could have thrown up so much dirt in so short a time.

When we had traversed the whole distance from Yorktown to the James River and back and had taken note of those places where so many of the New England soldiers slept in the mud,shoveled in the mud, ate in the mud, lived in the mud, and died in the mud,we stopped near the old cemetery and seated ourself on a knoll to rest. Our companion had bidden us good-night,and the sun was sinking among the trees in the west when we folded our arms under our head and leaned back upon the grass to recall the dark days of war, and in imagination to picture to ourself how the army appeared and what they did hereabouts six years ago. [Conwell was in the area about four days in June 1863 as a captain in the 46th Regiment, Massachusetts Infantry.]

We could readily see the muddy uniforms, the bright bayonets, the thin haversacks, the gray canteens, and the heavy knapsacks. We almost felt the chilly rains and the pestilential night winds, could see the hurrying officers and couriers, the picket guard and camp patrols,and hear the challenge of reliefs and officers of the day. We smiled to ourself as we thought of the rations in the cook-tents, the supper squads, the brigade drills when shoes that sank in the mud refused to come out, and of the remarks which the [observation] balloon ascensions called forth from the gossiping soldiery. We laughed outright, all alone, when we thought of the ridiculous camp rumors,the awkward squads, [Union] General [Fitz-John] Porter's [accidental] balloon ascension[and ride over Confederate lines], the fall in the soft mud of slick-uniformed officers, and the thousand and one stories which the boys related to us of this campaign when we camped together and heard the opprobrious epithet, "paper collars!"

We sighed,too,when we thought of the hard tasks, the spade work of the Engineer Corps, the poor rations, the absence of letters from home, the chills and fever,the sleepless nights, the feverish days, the sad scenes of the hospital, and the little mounds which rose beside each regimental row. We shed a tear as we remembered how the chaplain's sad letter to the friends [family or next of kin] went on its heart-rending mission, how the guard with reversed arms and muffled drum went to the grave,and how in the distant home the wife,or sister,or mother, or father was perchance enquiring that very evening, "Is there a letter from Willie?"

An old Negro who had been at work all day on his own land agreed to take us to Williamsburg that night if we "would go slow like," as his mule had worked hard all day. Williamsburg must be seen and it was our only chance,so we consented to "go slow," and clambered into his wagon. It was a better vehicle than the one in which we left Hampton, and we were satisfied, as at ten o'clock at night we started into the forest en route for Williamsburg.

We considered the price of the team extravagant, and so took in a passenger to share our seat and expense. But by the time we had gotten half a mile from town we heartily repented of our economical manœuver. For he began to shout and sing and cut pigeon-wings,exhibiting all the evidence of a growing state of intoxication. He was a short, heavy-bearded,flash-eyed Jew who came from Norfolk,Va., and visited Yorktown, as he said, to "look after dollas but found nodding but bad rum." For an hour he skipped about,leaping into the road and making the Negro driver wait for him to get in, or shouting to the mule and kicking the patient driver.

After a while, however, he became so much intoxicated that he could not rise from his seat, and with a few ineffectual attempts to stand, he fell down into the bottom of the wagon, dead drunk.

"I'm glad he's down, massa. I'se gettin short on it fur patience," said the driver, whipping up the mule.

"He is drunk," said we, "and drunken men are not responsible for what they do."

"I knowd it, I knowd it. I was only mad at the Satan that cum up from his abode to dwell in this man. He is a bad man anyhow, massa. He don't beliebe de Lord rose, and ob course de debil will hab him in some way or nudder. Bad sign, massa, berry bad sign, to be out sich a dark Friday night as dis am wid a misbeleeber."

"He is only a Jew, and they are God's chosen people," said we.

"Say nuffin' more, please, just nuffin' more, fur de devils dat walk in darkness will oberhear us," said our guide in a frightened tone, but it was so dark that we could not see either him or the mule.

"When will we get to Williamsburg?" asked we, after a long silence during which time we had rattled over stones, run against pine trees, splashed through brooks, and crushed through the dry branches of many a tree-top.

"Dun no, massa; maybe soon," said he in a half whisper, "but dis misbelieber ain't no good sign; de spirit of de Lord, dat led Mozais, may lead us to de end ob de longest road, maybe."

A few moments more of silence elapsed, when suddenly, as if he had received a deep wound, the drunken man at our feet gave a terrible shriek that echoed through the forest and made the cold chills run all over our body.

"For God's sake, massa, stop him. He wake de dead, I realy beliebe," gasped the Negro at the same time that we bent over the Jew to inquire what was the matter.

"Hell!" yelled he, in a wild, shrill tone that almost made our hair stand on end.

The Negro driver, evidently frightened out of his wits at the unearthly sound, which confirmed the worst of his superstitious fears, leaped from the wagon and dashed into the brush, making no reply to our earnest call through the darkness urging him to come back. We managed to stop the mule, although we could not find the reins, and lifting the Jew to the seat, asked him again what was the matter. He only muttered a few unconnected sentences about "money" and "rum" and threw his arms furiously about, nearly forcing us out of the vehicle.

What to do with him in a deep forest, on so dark a night, we could not determine, and cannot yet make up our mind what we should have done, had he not decided for us. After a few moans and several attempts to stand upright, he suddenly seemed possessed of a giant's strength, and pulling the seat from under us both, upsetting us into the bottom of the wagon box, he threw it at the mule with such force that it crashed into a hundred pieces. The startled mule, which had exhibited some uneasiness before, became uncontrollably frightened at this, and started up with such a bound that the Jew turned a somersault into the road, while the team, taking us with it, dashed off at lightning speed.

All our shouting and coaxing had no effect upon the affrighted mule and on we went like the wind, into the creeks and over ditches, while the tipping and swaying of the wagon prevented our rising to our feet. How far we had gone we cannot tell; but it was at least a ride of two minutes when the mule left the road and dashed into the brush and briars. Crash! crack! bang! over we went into a sea of dry pine brush, while the pieces of the wagon flew about our ears. On went the mule, crashing into the darkness, leaving us bewildered and half crazy in the prickly, thorny thicket. We at last sat down beside a large pine tree to wait till morning, and before the welcome light came we "resolved" at least a hundred times that it was no fun to be a correspondent. But our "resolutions," like those of the Sorosis [a women's club, founded in New York in 1868] availed us nothing, "for want of moral support."

In the morning, broken branches, bullet-pierced saplings and rails we found in every direction. At one place we noticed a beech tree a short distance from the road, bearing the following inscription cut in the bark: "J. W. F., 11th Mass."

[probably Major John W. Foye,a surgeon]. The tree
had grown considerably since the letters were carved
there, but the incisions were as distinct as the
plainest print.

WILLIAMSBURG

We came in sight of Williamsburg about 5 o'clock
in the morning. The town has an ancient look, reminding one of English villages where a jolly host
and a mug of beer always await the traveler. Many
of the buildings were destroyed during the war,
and their barren walls still stand, as the inhabitants say,as a reproach to the "vandal Yankees."
The College of William and Mary [chartered in
1693], which has educated Virginians including
Jefferson [1762], is now being rebuilt in the same
style as before,and while we were there a grammar
school already was occupying a part of the east
wing. [The College was closed during the Civil
War.]
The old [Bruton Parish]Episcopal Church[erected
1710-1715], overgrown with vines, bears the scars
of many a conflict;it had seen the funeral cortege
of many a noble captain during the Revolution and
was filled at the battle in [May] 1862,with hundreds
of bleeding soldiers. Its walls still bear the
marks of blood. The old Capitol building [at the
end of Duke of Gloucester Street] is gone [It was
restored after 1926 by gifts of money from John D.
Rockefeller, Jr. and Colonial Williamsburg, Inc.]
and only a small pile of bricks is left behind,
while the old Court House [of 1770] stands closed
and silent, casting a gloom over the buildings
around. We looked for the office where the first
newspaper [the *Virginia Gazette*] was published in
Virginia; but that, too, had disappeared. We
searched [near Jamestown] for the residence of
Sir William Berkeley, the [tyrannical colonial]
governor of Virginia, who [in 1671] thanked God
that there were no free schools or printing presses
in Virginia. [See Frank L.Mott's *American Journal-*
ism (New York: Macmillan Co., 1950), p. 6.] But
his house ["Green Spring"],like his theories, was
pulled down by the soldiers in 1863.
We could not fail to pause as we turned the corner

near the noble buildings of the insane asylum and looked back along the street noticing the aristocratic dwellings and antique business structures, and picturing to ourself the scene when the inhabitants fled from Williamsburg; when the college buildings, churches, and hotels were filled with Confederate dead and dying, and when the streets were blocked with every imaginable kind of vehicle, carrying household goods and women into the country; when the rebels ran through the town shouting,"The Yankees are coming!" and broke in and stole all that their friends had not taken; then the coming of the cavalry,infantry,and artillery of the Union Army, and the quiet occupation of the town.

Early in the afternoon, after looking at the still entire earthworks where[General Winfield S.] Hancock crossed the dam,and where[General John J.] Peck, [General William F.] Smith, and [General Joseph] Hooker threw up their entrenchments, we rode down the lines into the shattered woods, and in a short time reached Lee's Mill. Before, however, our attention was called to the spot where the 1st Massachusetts [Infantry] made their noble stand [on May 5, 1862]. Here [that same day] fell Newton's [in Massachusetts] first martyr, William Roger Benson, a noble young man, scarce 20 years of age and full of promise. [Formerly a clerk, he was a musician in Company I.] He said to his comrade,a few moments before being struck by the fatal bullet,"Tell the Colonel [Robert](Cowdin) if anything happens to me that I died fighting for my country faithfully to the last."

The graves of the fallen of the Massachusetts First Regiment were beautifully arranged in a small enclosure just at the edge of the battle-field, surrounded by a neat fence and under the shade of a spreading apple tree.

A VIRGINIA WEDDING

A wedding! a wedding! a wedding! a veritable wedding in old Virginia! A blooming daughter of an F. F. V. consents to wed a noble son of New Hampshire! When will wonders cease? Little did your correspondent think, when worrying down hash at the Spottswood [House] and cold pork at the

Exchange [Hotel, both hotels in Richmond], that in the short space of one week he should sit at a marriage feast. How much less did we think when our boots sank to the tops of Chickahominy [River] mud that we were "blacking" them for a wedding party. Yet such was the case. And now that the season of bliss has passed we feel as though we had lost something which only another wedding can restore. But, alas! we doubt if another such wedding will ever occur. Novelty, romance, patriotism, war, love, and privation add to the interest of this wedding, and Captain [Thomas M.] Reid [author of adventure stories popular with boys] and Sylvanus Cobb, Jr. [prolific New England novelist and short-story writer] may now stand aside, for the day has arrived when "truth is stranger than fiction."

The morning we arrived in Williamsburg in order to note the traces which were left of the Peninsular Campaign, we fell in with an old friend, J. S. Campbell, [formerly?] of New Haven [Connecticut], who insisted that we should accept a "general invitation" and go to a wedding. [Such announcements, even today, are published in some Southern newspapers.] At first we stoutly refused. For, after wandering for weeks among the battle-scarred trees and breastworks, with skulls, bones, graves, hobgoblins, and ghosts for our daily companions, the idea of a wedding was actually shocking. Then our dress! Our boots covered with yellow mud—our clothes whitened with the whitewash of cemetery fences, and so spotted that we were often reminded of Joseph's coat of many colors—our hat broken and dusty—all gave us the appearance of the halt, the poor, the lame, and the blind from the highways, rather than the invited guest with his wedding garment. But friendship and curiosity prevailed. Two miles into the country we tramped to witness the marriage, and on the way Mr. Campbell gave us the history of the happy parties.

When the 31st New York Regiment made its charge in the first fight [in June 1862] at White House [on the Pamunkey River] in McClellan's campaign, and before the gunboats came up to support them, one of the men was severely wounded in the right leg, and as our line of battle changed direction

he was left within the rebel lines. When he fell
he thought the wound so slight that he could get
up again at once.   But after repeated efforts he
found that he could not rise and was growing faint.
Twice the rebel skirmish line from the Hampton
command passed him, as he lay beside a pine bush,
without seeing him.   Fearing to be captured,   he
kept quiet,   although he was in great agony.   All
day he lay there pressing his bleeding wound with
his thumb,and hoping that his regiment would again
pass that way.   But the sound of firing indicated
that the fight was going farther and farther to
the northward,and he was left, whether within the
rebel lines or not he could not tell.

Night came, with its dews and damps [From Julia
Ward Howe's "Battle Hymn of the Republic," first
published in 1862,where the phrase is: " . . . in
the evening dews and damps."]chilling him through
and through, but no succor.   At last, beside himself with pain and thirst, he began to halloo for
assistance,   but through the long terrible night
no voice answered his call.   In the morning he
found himself sinking by degrees into a state of
insensibility and supposed he was dying.But while
he had sense enough left to know that he was living,
a girl about sixteen years of age passed the spot.
As soon as she saw him she shrieked with fright
and began to run away as fast as her feet could
carry her.   He managed to raise himself on his
elbow and with all his remaining strength shouted
after her,   "For God's sake, Miss, don't leave me
to die."

She heard him and stopped, hesitating whether
to go on or to return.   She looked toward the log
hut and then toward the pine bush,and finally came
slowly and hesitatingly back. That decision saved
the soldier's life.   When she reached the spot he
had fainted.   The ground where he lay was covered
with blood and his face was besmeared with the mud
in which he had writhed in his agony.   Sick and
faint at the sight of blood,   she tried to think
what she could do for the man;   and at the same
time she feared that when he became sensible he
might prove to be the monster she had heard the
Yankees were.   However,   her compassion overcame
all fear and hatred.   Something must be done for

him or his last words would haunt her all the days of her life. She would go to her father in the cabin. No! often had her father threatened to shoot the first Yankee he saw. No, no, she could not go to her father. After hesitating until she began to think the man was dead, she ran off into the woods and called an old Negro lady that was gathering fire wood. Together they returned and the old woman, who had "nussed many a sick un," proceeded to bathe the soldier's face and hands with water, while the girl gathered leaves to put under his head.But to make a long story short, they brought him to his senses, and after drinking some water he was able to sit up against the tree. They had to leave him there that night, for the girl's father and these two had fled from Williamsburg on its capture by our troops and had taken possession of that deserted log cabin for a temporary home "in the woods."

They had brought him, however, an old dress and a small blanket for a covering, and the next day, while her father was away, the girl and the Negro woman actually lugged the soldier half a mile to an old broken-down hovel, where they fed him for two days. Finally, after repeated solicitations from the wounded man, who felt his wound growing worse, they went all the way to our camp and told a picket of the condition of the soldier. Soon an ambulance, under guard, came and took him away. All this while the old fool of a refugee never had a suspicion that his daughter and the old servant were giving "aid and comfort" to the enemy, although their looks and acts must have been anything but calm.

Years passed on, as the novelist would say, and the war closed. The soldier, maimed for life, went to the Veteran Reserve Corps till the close of the war, we believe, and heard nothing from his benefactor for five years. At last, determined to find out what had become of her, he came down to Williamsburg from Nashua, N.H., where he was then at work, and after a two-days' search he found his white friend [then about twenty-one years of age], so changed, however, in appearance, that he did not know her. But the old black woman was dead.

We are not well enough versed in love affairs

to tell how they made love to each other and how, as our friend Campbell said, they proceeded as though love "was a matter of course."[Yet Conwell himself had been married four years!] But they soon became "engaged," although the old Yankee-hating refugee, still as much of a fool as ever, objected strongly to "any such nonsense." He "wouldn't hev the d—n Yankee within a mile o' the house," and if he came,this "indignant parent" would shoot him.

They carried on a correspondence through the Negroes and finally the young lady had the courage to tell her father that she would marry the soldier and "if he didn't like it he might lump it." This brought him to his senses somewhat, and as he had "no one else to 'pend on" he consented that the soldier might come to the house, and finally that they might marry if the soldier wouldn't take Miss Helen "up among the Yankees in New Hampshire." After a while they compromised the matter by agreeing to make their home near Madison, Wisconsin, where the soldier had some relatives. But her father still swore about the Yankees, and at times would get raving mad and say he "didn't suppose he was ever to be cussed with a d—n Yankee son-in-law." They say that "maids are best in battle woo'd" [Thomas Moore, "Lalla Rookh."] and we suppose it was so in this case!

But we must recall our thoughts, for the story has almost led us to forget the wedding. As Sylvanus [Cobb], Jr., would say, let us return to our hero.

The wedding took place in a rather small house, standing some distance from the highway, a huge brick chimney on the outside of each gable end. The darkeys for miles around had gathered in faint hopes of an old-time feast;while in little assemblies of five or six the lank,grisly-haired, mud-colored white men stood about the yard or hung their loose arms under the rail fence, actually too lazy to hold up their hands. On entering the parlor, to which we were cordially invited (after a peremptory order from the bride and bridegroom that their names should not be put in the papers), we found everything in readiness for the ceremony.

Soon the bride, dressed in a blue Thibet [fine wool] dress, with a faint imitation of a Grecian

Bend [body bent forward from hips—an 1869 fashion.
Popular in 1868-'69 was William H.Lingard's satir-
ical song, "The Grecian Bend." He also mentioned
the ridiculous mode in another song,"On the Beach
at Long Branch." That New Jersey resort was then
the summer residence of President Grant.] and the
bridegroom,dressed in black and limping on a cane,
came out of the next room arm-in-arm, accompanied
by a dozen or more young men and young ladies,the
latter "fussed up" in white. An old Southern back-
woods minister, whom we took to be a Quaker when
we went in,performed the ceremony,which he length-
ened out to a doleful length by prayers and exhortations. We supposed he was venting his spite on the
Yankee bridegroom,whose every appearance betrayed
his impatience for the end of the ordeal.
    At last it was over, and the kissing done, the
feast began. The bride passed the cake, cheese,
bread, etc., while her father straddled about the
assembly with whiskey, brandy, ale, etc.
    All the old stools, pots, kettles, and tables
were taken out of the kitchen into the yard, the
ashes brushed up into the fire-place, and an old
black fiddler placed upon a high bench in one
corner, and the dance began. Talk of the can-can
of Jardin-Mabille [in Paris], you who will! But
if you take exception to that,never go to a dance
in "Ole Virginny" and witness the Virginia Reel.
Such a calling,falling,sprawling,bawling,nipping,
skipping, slipping, ripping we never saw in Paris
[when we were there two years ago]. Hands up,
head up, feet up, mixed up! [Similar colorful
comments were expressed by author Samuel Clemens
the same year (1869) in his *The Innocents Abroad*
after he had watched—somewhat shocked— the Can-
Can a few months before. See the Stormfield
Edition, vol. I (New York: Harper & Brothers,
1929),pp.130-131.] Men laughing, women screaming,
fiddle screeching until at last, all out of time
and breath,they tumble into one mass of squirming
humanity. Then the men all take a drink and the
women fix their hair.
    After the first figure [we left], having some
fears for our health if we stayed and laughed any
more, and being more anxious to see the battle-
fields than the ball-room.

ROANOKE ISLAND

Many New England soldiers who have spent a portion of their war lives [as we have] upon the shores of North Carolina have wished they were able to make a visit to their old camping grounds and look again upon the scenes so full of thrilling interest. But the transition from war to peace has made such a change in the appearance of the fields and villages that the returning soldier can hardly realize they are the same. Leaving Virginia to which, however, we shall shortly return, we will wander along the Carolina coast and note for our comrades the changes that have been wrought since they came here to "fire the Southern heart." [This phrase was originated by Alabama's "fire-eater" statesman William L.Yancey (a brilliant and persuasive orator) when he wrote it in his nationally famous "scarlet letter" of June 15, 1858, from Montgomery to his friend, James Slaughter,on precipitating the cotton states into revolution.(See John C. Rives, "Senate Proceedings," *Appendix to the Congressional Globe*, Washington, 1st Session, 36th Congress, 1860, p. 313.) Yancey's full quotation is: "But if we could do as our fathers did—organize 'committees of safety' all over the cotton States (and it is only in them that we can hope for any effective movement) —we shall fire the Southern heart, instruct the Southern mind, give courage to each other, and, at the proper moment, by one organized, concerted action, we can precipitate the cotton States into a revolution." Compare with words (apparently a paraphrase of Yancey's),"fire the Northern heart," in William B. Hesseltine's "Life in the Confederacy: Confederate Prisons," *A History of the South 1607-1936*(New York: Prentice-Hall, 1936),p. 548).

The present appearance of Roanoke Island differs but little from that which it has worn for the past 200 years—a dreary waste of sand[part of the Outer Banks] covered in places with dwarf pines and briery marshes. Hard pressed by the necessities of life must the man be who to-day makes this desert his home. Yet it was here,and in the sixteenth century [1585] that high hopes of dominion were entertained by [Sir Walter Raleigh] the "pet lord" of England. Here, too, toiled the [first English]

colonists who, after years of suffering [between
1587 and 1591],concluded that either this was poor
soil, or they were very bad farmers; and here, by
the old lighthouse, as the darkey said, they "re-
spectfully took their leabins" [and became known
as "The Lost Colony"].

Its value as a military post, however, is not
governed by the depth of the sand,and the now empty graves of the patriots who fell attest the value
which Gen. Burnside put upon these sandhills. Here
were the hastily constructed forts and rifle pits
over which went [Colonel Rush C.] Hawkins' "Zous"
[Zouaves, of the 9th New York Infantry], and to
flank which the 21st, 23rd, 24th, 25th, and 27th
Massachusetts, with the 9th New Jersey, the 10th
Connecticut, the 4th and 5th Rhode Island, and the
51st [and 53rd] New York,waded to their eyes in the
ocean, crashed through the thorny thickets, and at
last,regardless of sharpshooters and rebel cannon,
carried at the point of the bayonet. It [February
8, 1862] was a terrible day. And a sad sight it
was,as the weary victory-crowned soldiers retraced
their steps to the shore,to see the dead stretched
on the beach and watch the stretchers and boards
that carried New England,New York,New Jersey, and
[the 51st] Pennsylvania heroes to their lonely
graves. But there was none of that feeling of sorrow and regret that the soldier knows when he car-
ries to his last resting place a comrade whose life
has won no victory.

But the ever-shifting sand and the spreading
thicket have left but little to tell where the fight
occurred, and the visitor who would to-day find
Forts Bartow, Forrest, Blanchard, or Huger must
look for other landmarks than the redoubts that once
pointed the way. Even the shell-broken trees have
disappeared, and the Negro villages, which teemed
with life during the war,are now nearly deserted,
and only a cabin here and there remains. The crumbling remains of the Federal fortifications which
were built to command the channel of Croatan Sound
are the only vestiges of war that would be recog-
nized by a stranger to the locality. Barren and
wild as ever, there is only one material change
since 1860. Then inhabited by a few ignorant fish-
ermen living in heathenish seclusion from every-

thing pertaining to civilization, to-day it can
boast of two schools—one for white and one for
colored children. The schoolmaster from Massachusetts is abroad, and, take our word for it, the
next generation will seek a more habitable locality. [Several soldiers from that State in 1862
started public schools for Negroes in eastern North
Carolina.]

PLYMOUTH

Shad! What soldier has been stationed at Plymouth and eaten no shad?There they lie—long rows
of the veritable shad—looking like the very same
fish we ate six years ago. [See Plymouth reports
in: Anon., "The 46th Regiment," (Northampton) *Gazette and Courier*, Aug. 11, 1863, p. 2; Capt.R.H.
C., "From the 46th Regiment," *supra*, May 19,1863,
p. 1; and April 28, 1863, p. 1.] Shad and hard
tack! Hard tack and shad! Deliver us from ever
seeing the like again! We will rejoice, too, that
the day is passed when [Confederate] General[George
E.] Pickett—who stood in his own door last week
[in Richmond where he was manager of the Virginia
agency of Washington Life Insurance Company of New
York] and ridiculed us about it—can come down upon us [as he did at Newport Barracks in 1864] and
"gobble us up," taking us to the land where comfort and shad are unknown. No danger now of capture, for the [gunboats USS] *Miami* and *Southfield*
[active at Plymouth from April 17 to 20, 1864] are
gone after the shad; the blackened timbers of the
rebel gunboats just show above the muddy Roanoke
[river]; Forts Warren and Wessels are a ruin; and
there is not life enough in Plymouth to catch a
rheumatic flea. At the close of the year a few
Massachusetts officers thought they would invest
their capital in Plymouth and astonish the people
with their Yankee way of doing business, and they
did astonish, not only the natives but everybody
else with their *modus operandi* and the remarkably
short space of time in which they managed to spend
their money and "fail up."
But the present appearance of Plymouth is dull
and uninteresting. A short walk to the fortifica-

tions now washing away, a glance over the cultivated fields covered with fallen timber during the
war, and a cordial greeting with a few old acquaintances, and the visitor asks for the stage.* Few
men are to be seen on the streets, and our friends
say that there are but few here, nearly all in the
forest cutting timber or in the fields cultivating
cotton or corn. Some of the old houses, with shot
holes in their roofs, and old hats in the windows,
look somewhat familiar, but a darkey says: "Gwaune
up country, sar," and off we go to Rainbow Bluff
[now called Rainbow Banks] almost wishing we had
never made the trip. [All we found was the remains
of a Confederate earthwork fort on the hundred-
foot cliffs (bluffs) near Williamston on the Roa-
noake River.]

LITTLE WASHINGTON

The village at the head of Pamlico Bay was called
Little Washington by soldiers in 1863-64 [to dis-
tinguish it from the national capital], but it is
a very much *smaller* Washington now. The old houses
have been torn down or destroyed by fire; all the
army buildings have been removed; and a most insignificant place it is, hardly worth mention but
for the interesting incidents which occurred there.
The line of earthworks around the town and the batteries "down the river" are still in a good state
of preservation and remind one strongly of the "in-
conveniences" to travel on the river in March, 1863.
But the gunboats that so gallantly ran the block-
ade, and by which General Foster managed to relieve
the needs of the besieged army, are gone, together
with all the paraphernalia of war; and one or two
oyster scows are the only reminders of the [gunboat
USS] *Ceres,* the [United States transport steamer]
Escort, and the gay flotilla of '63. Negroes now
loaf about the old guard quarters, and pallid North
Carolinians now oversee the work of their wives in
gardens planted on the "old camp ground." [Walter
Kittredge, "Tenting on the Old Camp Ground."] With

---

*Either a stagecoach or station for change of horses.

no [travelers'] accommodations, many old landmarks removed, and inhabited by a Yankee-hating element that cannot be blamed as they know no better, Washington has little to attract the visitor, and even an old soldier's first thought is, as he lands in town, "Which is the best road out?"

NEWBERN

Newbern [A common spelling in the Civil War era —sometimes also spelled Newberne. The city's name is now spelled New Bern, two words, honoring its Swiss origin.] in war surrounded by tented camps, long lines of earthworks and forts, with a fleet of gun-boats floating in the Neuse River, was a far different city from the Newbern of to-day. It seems to have been reduced in size, until it is but a miniature of the city we knew five years ago [when, as captain in the 2d Regiment, Massachusetts Heavy Artillery, we were stationed in the Fort Totten-Fort Macon area].

Then there was a constant tramp of soldiers along the side-walks, sentries on every corner, and jolly crowds in every tradesman's door. Now business is dull and the streets seem almost deserted. The wharves, that once creaked under the loads of ordnance and quartermasters' stores, where happy-faced sutlers and town merchants received their goods, and soldiers their boxes from home, are now occupied by colored dealers in fish and oysters. The substantial army wagons and ambulances that were constantly moving through the streets are replaced by a few two-wheeled carts, drawn by lame mules or "dwarfed cows" [Perhaps Conwell's roguish metaphor for steers.], appearing as little like the noble beasts we formerly saw here as their drivers do like healthy or prosperous men.

The sight of the traveller is refreshed, however, at long intervals, by the appearance of a horse and buggy belonging to some aristocratic North Carolinian or enterprising Yankee. The hospital buildings, so sadly familiar to many of our soldiers, have lost that appearance of quiet and gloom they had during the war, and now, as schoolhouses or dwellings, look cheerful and inviting. Whole

blocks of buildings have been destroyed by fire,
and in many places new structures, of a different
style, have taken the places of old ones.
Without the city the change is greater than within. The broad fields, once so white with tents,
and the parade grounds,once covered with drilling
battalions,are now cultivated by the plough or are
left to grow to brush or barren weeds. On the spot
where were encamped the 46th and 8th Massachusetts
[Regiments] in '63 the National Cemetery now stands,
a sad memento of battles and disease. [It has 3,276
graves, 1,091 of unknown soldiers.] Fort Totten,
considered in the confident days of '64 one of the
strongest fortifications on the coast,has crumbled
away, and the huge piles of sand, which remain of
the lofty traverse, remind us forcibly of some
ruined castle that has been crumbling for five hundred years.

The line of earthworks reaching from Fort Totten
to the [Neuse and Trent] rivers on either hand, has,
in many places,entirely disappeared,while in other
localities portions of it remain entire. The hands
of nature and of men are fast destroying the landmarks of the war, and in a few years more not a
mound or ditch will be left to tell of the exhaust-
ing toils and wearing sieges endured by the soldiers of New England. Yet, with all the change,
there are many familiar localities and buildings in
the city which recall the experiences of camp life:
the large white house in which [Union] General
[John G.] Foster had his headquarters; the long
flag staff on an adjacent corner; the medical dis-
pensary; the old railroad depot; the now dilapidated and dangerous bridge across the Trent River;
and the low house occupied by Chaplain [Captain
Horace] James [25th Massachusetts Infantry Regi-
ment] and his corps of teachers; the numerous Negro
huts beside the Trent, where were encamped for a
long time the 27th, the 23d, and the 21st Massachusetts, and the 9th New Jersey; the remnants of barracks near the Neuse once occupied by the 23d,17th,
43d, and 44th Massachusetts; the steamer *Ellen S.
Terry*, on which usually came those welcome letters
from home and which still plies between this port
and New York; and the old post office building,on

the corner,still used for that purpose. All with
the many offices,guard quarters, and store houses
bring again a realization of former army life.
But the National Cemetery,with its array of white
headboards bearing the names of many an old friend
and fellow laborer,is the surest and saddest prompt-
er of memory which the place affords. Drummer boys
who beat the reveille in time of quiet, and the
long roll in the hour of danger,and who went safely
through the Virginia campaigns, were conquered by
yellow fever here. A sergeant,honored for his in-
tegrity and praised for his bravery [in battles] at
Plymouth and Roanoke [both in eastern North Caro-
lina] lies here almost forgotten. Private soldiers
—our schoolmates and old acquaintances—fallen in
battle or sickness, are placed here, as their headboards tell us, until the Resurrection Day. At one
end of a row are two graves,of which uncommon care
has been taken, and to which our attention was
called by the keeper.One bears the following touching inscription:

No. 1744
21st Massachusetts
Betrothed to C.E.C.

(The name is not given on the board,but we learned
that it was a member of Company E, of this regiment.) [Massachusetts Adjutant General's reports
for Co. E show a Lieutenant Charles Coolidge, of
Sterling,died of disease at New Bern on March 30,
1862.]
The other reads as follows:

Miss Carrie E. Cutter
Betrothed to No. 1744
Buried at His Side at Her Own Request

Probably many in the old 21st will know the circumstances and tell the story of these two lovers;
but the inscription on their headboards is all we
know of their life of love or devotion at death.
When we look over the names of our acquaintances
who are buried here and think how, with a few exceptions,all our old schoolmates have fallen in war,
and how desolate and cheerless are their homes away

among the mountains of Western Massachusetts [Conwell and many of his war comrades were reared in Hampshire County.]; how the little old church is filled with orphans and weeping widows; how the land that once "blossomed as the rose" is now barren for the need of the hands that once tilled it; how the little children, whose memory is limited to a few years, ask, day after day, why they have no father, and why their mother is crying over her work; how the little old mill on the foaming stream is as silent as the voice of its owner; how gloomy the streets that once rang with laughter, and how like a funeral the whole landscape about our mountain home [at South Worthington, Massachusetts] appears, we cannot avoid asking the questions: Was such a sacrifice needed? Why does the God of Justice permit the men who brought on this fearful war to go free and unpunished, petted and honored, apparently as happy as though their actions had not flooded the land with blood? But let us turn from the sad things of the past to the more cheerful present and leave the cemetery in charge of its maimed keeper, who has promised us a complete list of the men from our own State who lie there.

North Carolina, as well as Virginia, has its quota of Yankees who assist materially in filling up the State Legislature and government offices. Hundreds of men whose first acquaintance with the State was made during the war are now permanently established in business here. In Newbern about every live business man you meet is from the North, and we are sorry to say that nearly all of the men we knew have "failed" once or twice since the close of the war. But with Yankee perseverance, they begin again, and the promises of better times coming seem in a fair way to be fulfilled. Captains and lieutenants whom we once saw touching their caps in a careless way at the salute of well-drilled guards are now packing fish, running a hotel, shipping freight, or making long speeches and taking large drinks in the State Legislature at $7 per day.

Among the liveliest and most prosperous New England men we found here were the Kilbourne brothers of White Bros. & Kilbourne, and Mr. M.M. Rutter of the Boston & North Carolina Tar and Turpentine Company. These gentlemen are from Boston and show their enterprise by taking [that is subscribing to] the *Traveller*. Cambridge, Dedham, Somerville, Salem, Haverhill, and Worcester [all in Massachusetts] are represented by ex-soldiers in business here, while one of Springfield's [also in Massachusetts] noble sons, Mr. Frank Stearns, conducts the editorial department of the Newbern *Daily Times*. One of the colored aldermen, whom we saw driving an old mule cart along the street, has the appearance of an "intelligent contraband," and would be an excellent personification of a moonless midnight in an allegorical tableau. [Shelley, Percy B., "La̅on and Cythna (The Revolt of Islam)," c̅anto XI, sta̅nza viii, line 1: "Woe! woe! that moonless midnight —." See Forman, Harry B., *The Works of Percy Bysshe Shelley*, vol. 1 (London: Reeves & Turner, 1880), p. 278].

The "boys" will remember with what scorn they were treated by the ladies of Newbern when the troops first arrived here, and in many cases this contempt for the Yankees was kept up until the city was entirely free from Federal troops. One of the most insolent women and one who could not rest unless she had insulted the "invading Yankee," at last, by those strange freaks of Cupid, fell in love with a Yankee captain, who since the war had taken up his abode at a near neighbor's. She felt that she was fast reaching that uncertain age beyond which unmarried ladies should never go, and she was at last willing to abandon her prejudices, provided she could get a fine-appearing, handsome husband. A few months ago they were married, with all the pomp of a Southern marriage. But, alas! on the second day of the honeymoon the bridegroom was nowhere to be found and has not been heard from to this day. The disconsolate bride, however, consoles herself with the idea:

> Better be courted and jilted
> Than not be courted at all.

[Thomas Campbell, "The Jilted Nymph."]

And she says that "No Yankee will come any more games" over her, "you bet." There is such a combination of justice and injustice in this case that we hardly know whether to laugh or mourn! A Yankee miller, who has recently constructed a mill on the Trent River, about two miles from Newbern, has recently made a most wonderful discovery. While digging a channel for the [mill's] raceway, he came upon a fine bed of marl in which were found the bones of an animal that must have been much larger than the mastodon. The sections of the vertebrae which he brought to town were over eleven inches in diameter, while the rib bones were twelve feet in length. Some of the latter were petrified. We should be pleased to have Prof. [Louis] Agassiz [of Harvard University] tell us to what monster species this specimen belongs. There is no "humbug" about this [The Agassiz "humbug" anecdote is related in Henry Blake, "Personal Reminiscences of Professor Louis Agassiz," *Nature-Study Review* 19 (1923), p. 100.], for all parts of the animal's frame are being discovered and are well worth the attention of scientific men and students of natural history.

After crossing the Trent River on our way to Beaufort [pronounced Bó-furt] and Fort Macon, we passed the ruins of the old breastworks and blockhouses which are so familiar to the members of the 23d, 21st, 27th, and 43d Massachusetts, and in a half-hour found ourselves on the old Newbern Battle-field. Here the trees which were felled in front of the batteries and over which the 21st [Massachusetts Infantry] was charging at the time [First Lieutenant Frazer A.] Stearns, of Amherst [Massachusetts, member of Company I], was killed [March 14, 1862] have been turned up, the trunks rolled together, and the field burned over preparatory to cultivation. The line of rebel earthworks remains entire and, being nearly overgrown with young trees, will doubtless remain for ages to mark the spot where was fought one of the severest battles of the war. The Negroes who are engaged in "chipping" the pine trees for turpentine will readily guide the visitor to the [earth] works.

DOWN TO FORT MACON

Between the Newbern Battle-field and Newport Barracks [about thirty miles southeast] there is little of interest, unless it be the mounds at Croatan, which are what is left of the old rifle pits, and the ruined block-house at Havelock. The locality called Batchelder's Creek, so well known to every soldier who has been stationed at Newbern, has been entirely abandoned and is fast returning to the primitive forest. The ruins of the old blockhouses and the camp of the Pennsylvanians are still discernible, but of all the cabins and tents that once filled the opening, only one dilapidated hut remains. The Negroes have searched every ravine and earthwork thoroughly for old iron and have found it a very profitable business. A farmer from Cambridge [Massachusetts], who has settled on a fine farm between this point and Newbern, informs us that the darkeys would consider it an infringement on their rights for a white man to carry off the old pieces of shell, &c., even from their own land. That right and the idea that "Massa Grant" [now President] is going to give them all a piece of land cannot be argued out of their minds.

At Newport Barracks several of the old log buildings used for barracks and the line of earth works built in 1864 remain. [Conwell, a captain, was stationed at the Barracks during the winter of 1863-1864.] Beyond the fort a large field is under cultivation. The old "secesh" merchant still keeps a little store at Newport, and the ruins of the fort there can still be seen. They say the logs of the old block-house and other works at the outpost on Bogue Sound have entirely disappeared. At Morehead City and Beaufort the visitor can see but little change, as they were not occupied by troops to any great extent during the War. The hospitals [including Hammond General at Beaufort] have been transformed into hotels and dwellings.

At Fort Macon the signs of sieges and battles are still visible. The scarred parapets and shell-pierced walls tell over again the story of [General Ambrose E.] Burnside's "one day of siege" [April 26, 1862]. The old sand hills a short distance up the island are pointed out to-day as the spot where he placed the heavy guns that caused the old fort to crumble and its proud inmates to surrender, who but the day before laughed in scorn and wrote to their friends that they would "die to a man" before the fort would be surrendered. The fort is in neat order now and is garrisoned with the same scrupulous discipline that it was through the years of war. [Conwell's heavy artillery company was headquartered there 1863-1864.] The appearance of the harbor [at Morehead City and Beaufort] had undergone a greater change than any of its surroundings. When we were stationed here [from 1862 to 1864] the harbor was usually well filled with vessels of every size and shape. The grim old man-of-war, the sharp cutter, the flat gun-boat,and the monitor,with here and there the grey hull of some captured blockade-runner of English pattern, made the bay a lively scene to look upon. But to-day scarcely a sail is seen, and little canoes and oyster boats glide about where the terrible "kings of the sea" [Matthew Arnold,"The Forsaken Merman."]once lay at anchor. The government tug, with its little flag at the stern,is the only vessel left of all that numerous fleet,and consequently the harbor appears deserted and lonely. The fleet, the tents, the army, and the flags are gone, and the only companions we recognize are the huge waves among which we have often picked up beautiful shells,and whose voices will still call us a thousand years to come. "Roll on, thou deep and dark blue Ocean—roll!" [George Gordon, Lord Byron, " Childe Harold's Pil- grimage."] And thanks be unto Him whose hand con- trols the wave,no hostile fleet now rides upon thy breast.

FORT FISHER

It was a bright, beautiful morning when we left Wilmington [North Carolina] to visit Fort Fisher. The banks of the Cape Fear River, down which the tug boat hurried us, were covered with verdure, and all nature seemed to be in bloom. Rarely have we ever enjoyed a more pleasant voyage, seen more beautiful flowers, or more inviting shades. The beautiful wild roses on the plantation at Fort Anderson, the twining vines of brilliant green, and the songs of the dazzling red birds [cardinals?] reminded us of the beautiful rivers of France and Italy [which we saw two years ago], although there the charm is caused by the artificial regularity of the landscapes, and here by their natural diversity. American scenery can scarcely be compared with European; as the one is wild and untutored, while the other is cultivated and trimmed. But to us the natural beauty of our own land is nearly as far above the scenic beauty of Europe as the natural works of God are above the unnatural works of man. In Italy the landscapes are soft and soothing; here thet are beautifully wild, stirring, and grand. As we gazed upon the shores during that thirty miles of travel, and again as we heard the loud waves crash and roar about the hills of Fort Fisher, we were more in love than ever with our own favored land.

Directly in the mouth of the Cape Fear River stands a large island around which the divided river passes to the ocean. These two branches are the inlets through which ships [bound] for Wilmington must pass. The southern inlet is commanded by Fort Caswell and an old National fortification, and the northern by Fort Fisher, a work erected during the war. The latter is on the point [Federal Point] of the main land where the river and ocean unite, and all vessels must pass for a long distance under its guns before reaching the channel between the submerged banks of sand. Here it was that the great Battle of Fort Fisher took place [January 15, 1865], so well and so sadly known to all our readers. Here it was at a high sand hill known as Battery [or Fort] Buchanan that our colored boatman carried us on his back through the foaming waves to the low shore, leaving a youth to drag the [skiff] boat over the sand bars to the dry land.

We were somewhat surprised at the appearance of the fort, as we had expected to see a square fortification, protected on all sides by heavy works, and had supposed that the works were constructed in the usual manner. But instead of an entire enclosure, the works occupy only two sides of a square, one front being [eastward] toward the sea and the other toward the main land, with nothing whatever to protect it from the river and bay behind. The fort is of such prodigious proportions that the traverses appear in the distance like a lofty range of moun-

tains; and verily they are artificial mountains of
timber and sand. For a mile and a half along the
shore they rise one after another, and so near together that they unite at the base about 20 feet
above the level of the plain.

In these huge crevices, where they unite, were
planted the heavy guns which [the North Atlantic
Squadron, commanded by Rear Admiral David Dixon]
Porter, after the discharge of five thousand shells,
managed to silence. While standing upon these high
mounds, seventy feet or more above the sea, a fine
view is gained of the ocean and of the forts across
the bay and river. How it was possible for man to
build this lofty range of hills with the spade is
to us a matter of wonder and seems to rival the besiegers of Tyre [led by Alexander in 332 B.C.] who
began at a distance and shovelled a mountain [prob-
ably a causeway or mole] before them up to the very
walls of that city [on the eastern shore of the
Mediterranean Sea].

The superiority of sand over stone, in the construction of heavy fortifications, is here demonstrated. For almost entire the work still remains,
although the walls of [Forts] Sumter [at Charlestown,
South Carolina] and Pickens [near Pensacola, Florida]
crumbled to dust before a less severe bombardment
than these mounds received.

We say they stand entire—but we mean, however,
as far as the agency of man is concerned; for the
active waves of old ocean are fast undoing the proud
work of man, and all along the sea face the hills
are sliding gradually into the encroaching waves.
The [high] Mound Battery, which stands out alone
near the point, has fallen away, until its heavy
timbers, which composed the carriage platforms,
now project out over the water, and the remaining
sand beneath them will soon go to its native reefs,
and they be launched in the ocean for a long and
unknown voyage.

The provisions, ammunition, and stores which were
once packed away in the corners of these hollow
hills have been removed, but the traveller can
still walk upright in those gloomy recesses and
feel the same cool circulation of air in which the
soldiers of the besieged citadel so often refreshed
themselves. The log-celled casemates—from the

portholes of which the Confederates pointed their Armstrong guns of English make and in which our troops afterward stabled their horses—are still entire and furnished a cool and welcome retreat from the rays of the sun for this weary and foot-sore correspondent.

Only one building now remains of that large city of barracks and tents which before and after the surrender adorned the parade grounds. That was formerly occupied by an unfortunate darkey who, according to our [colored] boatman, while engaged in hunting for old iron, was blown up by a shell, which he struck with an axe, and the pieces of whom, according to the same informant, were harder to find than bullets, as he was "blowed into eetle shrimps of nuffin." His successor, a careful man, married the disconsolate widow, including the house, of course, and the neat little garden near it, and whenever he visits the shore, he always goes a long distance around the spot where his unfortunate pred-ecessor met his sad fate.

> Ay, me! What perils do environ
> The man that meddles with cold iron!
> [Samuel Butler, *Hudibras*.]

The stumps of the demolished stockade [palisades], which covered the [northeastern] land front of the fort and which was simply a row of timbers driven into the ground close together and sharpened at the top, are still to be seen above the drifts of sand and show what perilous work it must have been for [Brevet Brigadier General Newton M.] Curtis's Bri-gade to hew them down with axes, under fire of the Confederate troops above them. The large tract be-yond the stockade, and near the sea shore, once oc-cupied by the graves of a thousand dead, is now covered with banks of drifting sand. The bodies have all, or nearly all, been removed to the Wil-mington [National] Cemetery. [There lie 2,290 dead, 1,577 unknown.]

In the catalogue of the World's Greatest Heroes should the names be written of those men who fought or fell at this place. To charge a mile over a level plain in the face of canister-shotted cannon and a double line of rifles; to stop in the shower of lead and with axes hew down a stockade of logs ten or twelve inches in diameter;then seize their guns and rush across the ditches and up the precipitous side of an unstable sand hill; and,after clambering up forty feet, be met by the bayonets of the enemy pointed in a long line down above their heads; to see their wounded comrades roll down the sand bank to the stagnant pool; to seize the bayonets of the enemy with the left hand and thrust him through with the musket in their right; to tumble their foes down into the interior and rush, in the sliding sand, unhesitatingly down after him and then conquer and capture him is a work no one will envy, and for which no patriot can withhold from them the praise so justly their due.

We have heard it remarked that the soldiers, doubtless, loved such fights. But we have yet to see the one who did. Soldiers were men! They thought as much of safety and valued their lives as highly as other men. They were afraid, and trembled as a fight came on,and nothing but their lofty sense of duty and natural pride would lead them to face a cannon. If they loved a fight, and it was fun to charge on a fort, then there was no sacrifice made and no display of patriotism. The man that dreads the battle and trembles at the conflict and yet goes unhesitatingly on is the patriotic, brave man. But he who finds amusement in it is merely a reckless dare-devil and deserves no more sympathy when wounded than the man who jumped overboard in a storm for the fun of frightening the crew. Ah, no! Talk to the "Home Guards" when you would tell about "spoiling for a fight," and not to old soldiers. [See Frank Moore's *Rebellion Record,* 1861, vol. I, issue 3, p.8.] Only post clerks and Gallups Island [in Boston harbor] bounty-jumpers will ever tell you about the "glory" and "fun" of charging up to the cannon's mouth. The men who fell here were noble, valuable men. Their lives were worth much to themselves and to their country. Yet they made the sacrifice. Let their names be enrolled among

> ...the few, the immortal names
> That were not born to die.
> [Fitz-Greene Halleck,"Marco Bozzaris."]

From the top of the highest mound the ocean can be seen for many miles, as it foams and whirls over the sandbars, dotted here and there by the dismantled wreck of some blockade-runner, rebel ram, or iron-clad which went down during the war and is now being washed upon the shallows by the unceasing action of the waves. The ship channel, which at the time of the bombardment was nearly opposite the angle of the fort, has since shifted far to the south-ward, and the neat white light-house, erected within the fort a few months ago, is now far out of range with the channel. We suggested to the keeper that it should be placed on wheels in order to follow the channel, but he was not sufficiently posted on navigation to know whether the light-house was erected to be a guide for shipping or to keep the crows from eating corn.

We are more convinced than ever of the utter uselessness of an attack on this fort by General Butler with the force he had with him at the time [December 25, 1864] he attempted to land. [He actually did land, as a test, three thousand men a few miles above the fort but soon re-embarked them.] That our troops would [suffer] and must have suffered a disastrous defeat, and many a family been in mourning that is now proud and happy in the society of friends, is a conclusion forced on us when we look over the ground and consider the circumstances attending that attempt. Few men would have dared to put back without a fight. Most men would rather have sacrificed a thousand or two of lives than meet the finger of scorn pointed by the hand of a mistaken public. But history will set all things right. The credit which General Butler receives will not, however, detract in the least from the honor and glory won [in the capture of the fort] by his successor, General [Alfred H.] Terry, or by the troops under his command. [Terry landed eight thousand men January 13, 1865, and the fort fell two days later.]

While we were examining the traces left of Terry's fortifications on the peninsula above the fort and endeavoring to ascertain where the landing was made, we fell in with a "Confedrit sojer," who, in a discussion upon the comparative patriotism of the armies, told us the following queer story:

When the battle [March 19-21,1865] near Bentonville [North Carolina] was progressing, a rebel battery[from Johnston's army]getting out of ammunition charged [that is,loaded] their pieces with everything they could get. Two Yankee soldiers of Irish birth [from a wing of Sherman's army] who were "skedaddling" stopped behind a large tree to rest. While there a large hammer, fired by the aforesaid battery,came crashing through the trees, and stopped just in front of them. Shortly afterward a raid of tongs followed the hammer,and then an anvil sailed through the air and fell. When they heard the crash of the last named missile and saw it drop near its predecessors,one of them leaped excitedly to his feet exclaiming:

"Jeems, Jeems! be me sowl we must be afther laving. Der yer sa their slidge and their toongs and their arnveel? Be jabers, Jeems, their blacksmeeth's shoop will be after coomin nixt!"

Our Confederate friend related the story, with a great deal of gusto, to show how the Yankees skedaddled while the rebels stuck by until every available missile was fired away. We laughed at the joke, but demurred to its truthfulness—which so offended our new acquaintance that, fearing he might order "pistols for two" if we stayed in his society longer,we thanked him for his information and walked down the beach.

We passed the night after leaving Fort Fisher at the house of an old army acquaintance in Smithville [down the river opposite Fort Caswell], where the rebels had a fort [Fort Johnston] and where a company of the 8th U.S. Infantry is now stationed. Our friend, like all the Northern people we have seen, wishes himself back in Massachusetts; for there is no money, no society, no business here, and he stated, with emphasis, that a man having a bare subsistence with New England advantages was richer than a man here with a fortune. Every Yankee seems to fail in making money here; and all are selling out that can get enough money to return.

FORT CASWELL

From Smithville we visited Fort Caswell, which formerly was a fine old fort commanding the southern inlet, but the rebels at the capture of Fort Fisher blew it up and broke the gun carriages so that it is nothing but a ruin now. The heavy guns for some reason were not removed when Fort Fisher was dismantled and still lie among the broken timbers, rusty and useless. We noticed an old building, the roof of which had fallen in, and was told that our troops used it for a hospital. We also visited a fisherman's camp near the fort, and there saw the "company range," with the accompanying pots and kettles, which formerly belonged to some Union soldiers. It was in full blast and reminded us of the hard-tack mush, the soup, and boiled horse which kept the soldiers up to the fighting weight. As we stood looking at the familiar kettles, it seemed as though we could almost hear the sergeant's order, "Fall in, boys! fall in for rations!" and the lively rattle of tin plates and coffee cups as the boys in disordered fatigue dress, some without hats, others without shoes, fell hastily into line, and joking and grumbling, carried their rations to their "bunks."

FORT ANDERSON

But the waiting boat and rising tide admonished us that we must go, and reluctantly we turned from the familiar kettles at the call of the boatman waiting to take us up the river to Fort Anderson. When we reached the fort the steamer for Wilmington was in sight, and our survey of the spot was necessarily hasty. The ruins of an old church still stand near the fort, shattered and worn, with the ivy, planted by some devoted hand, still clinging to the masonry. Beside the church is a graveyard. But some one, supposing no doubt that the persons buried there in 1717 had been favored with headstones long enough, has removed them from the old yard and set them at the head of Confederate graves in an adjoining field. The use of old gravestones bearing the 1717 inscriptions for new graves of 1865 is an act of economy of which we have never

before heard. But as the land for ten miles around
is owned by one man and neither he nor his vassals
can read, we presume the old marble answers every
practical purpose.
The fort itself is a large earthwork and appears
as gloomy and threatening as ever. [It was captured
by Union troops February 18, 1865.] The cannons,
however, have all been removed by the Government,
and the land about the work is now being planted
with cotton by a Negro, who pays $2.50 rent for
each acre, when $3.00 would buy it outright—and
some land sells for 50 cents an acre. The colored
race have hardly found their level yet. Our conversation with the colored farmer was cut short
by the arrival of the [fifty-five ton, screw-
propelled] steamer, and leaping into a [ship-to-
shore] boat we were soon alongside the [Philadelphia-
built] *Alpha*, in which we returned to Wilmington
[up the Cape Fear River].

CHARLESTON

"Charleston!" says the conductor [of the North
Eastern Railroad train].
Charleston! Can it be? We? a Yankee? a mudsill?
[In the building trade, a very low structural com-
ponent.] a dirty mechanic? a Negro worshipper? a
hated invader? despoiler of the fair South? burner
of peaceable dwellings? insulter of harmless women?
blood-thirsty devil? a vagabond, and a member of
the Northern hordes? Can it be that the foot of
the hated Yankee is to tread the sacred soil of
South Carolina, and no avenging hand be there to
stay his march and rid the air of his polluting
presence?

Ye gods! Can such things be?

[Probably adapted from William Shakespeare's *Mac-
beth*, III, 4.]
Where are the defenders of the slave-holding republic who joined hands around [John C.] Calhoun's
grave [in Charleston] and swore to defend secession
or die—making, however, the mental reservation,
"if they liked the business"? Where are [Robert
B.] Rhett (alias Smith), [Robert] Toombs, [Charles]
Memminger, [William] Yancey, [Francis] Pickens,

[Jefferson] Davis,[David] Jamison,[William]Miles, [James] Orr, [John] Inglis, who stated that the "Southern chivalry" could whip three to one of the ignorant hirelings of the North? Where are the "Palmetto Guards"[Charleston volunteers];the women and children that "would die in the last ditch"; the torchlight processions,with their motto: "The Union Is Dissolved?" Where are the secession bonnets [also called Palmetto cockades],the Palmetto flags; the gay decorations? The high liberty pole bearing aloft the motto: "Animis Opibusque Parati" ["Ready in Soul and Resource"] and under which should have been written, "Quos Deus vult perdere prius dementat" ["Those whom God wishes to destroy He first deprives of their senses."]? Where are the mustering armies; the heavy cannons,the wagon trains of ammunition, and the thousands of people who crowded the housetops and wharves,and with gay flags and white handkerchiefs encouraged the besiegers of Fort Sumter [April 12-14,1861]? Awake! "The Philistines be upon thee!" [Judges 16:9.]

No sound. No answer. They are gone. Even the halls in which they concocted treason have disappeared and their ashes enrich the soil of a Negro freedman. The squares, around which paraded the procession [December 20,1860] celebrating the Ordinance of Secession,are piled with hideous ruins, and the mocking walls of church and cathedral answer the prayers they once heard for God's blessing on the aristocracy. As if Providence guided the missiles of war, the large white [O'Connor] house with its lofty column-supported porch, in which the Yankee [officer] prisoners were placed "under fire" [of Union guns from Morris Island], stands out majestically from the ruin and ashes with which it is entirely surrounded.

The [South Carolina] Military Academy[alias"The Citadel"] from which issued the cadets who fired the first gun[in the Civil War at the Union steamer *Star of the West*] is now filled with uniforms of another color,for the "Yankee hirelings" [Federal troops] have been garrisoned there [since 1865]. The houses of the aristocracy are marred by pieces of shell and the shot-pierced roofs of the city buildings,including the jail in which the Federal prisoners were confined, are patched and leaky. The columns on the Custom House which fell before the storm of iron [in 1863], from [Fort] Wagner and the "Swamp Angel"[an eight-inch Parrott gun], the dilapidated wharves, all tell of treason and its legitimate results. Well might they, when stirring up the wrath of a great and free people, have quoted from the great poet [Alexander Pope, in his "The Iliad of Homer"]:

The day shall come, the great avenging day,
Which Troy's proud glories in the dust shall lay,
When Priam's pow'rs and Priam's self shall fall,
And one prodigious ruin swallow all.

But the Charlestonians will not admit that the shells set anything on fire and claim that all this destruction of property was caused by the careless-ness of a "d—d nigger." Yet somehow the city is burned and the shot holes are still seen. The men, too, are gone. Many of the leaders never lived to see the end. Many others are in exile, and many are penniless that once commanded thousands. [Fervent secessionist] Edmund Ruffin, who fired [one of] the first guns of the war, committed suicide [June 15, 1865]. One of the commanders of the [Confederate] "Floating Battery," whose fortunes like the battery, split and floated out to sea, is now in South America a "voluntary exile," and asking General Grant [now President] if he "may come home." [About ten thousand Southerners became expatriates.] The slaves of 1860 now "insult" the chivalry by asking for pay. The land sharks must sell out their land to pay the taxes. The Yankee soldiers now parade the streets, and numerous National flags float above the city. The General Orders of [General] Beauregard [commanding at Charleston] have ceased to be posted. Blockade-runners come from treacherous England no more. The army has come home. The Yankees are settling in the city. The great Confederacy is "gin out" [Then-current dialect for given up, fallen, or surrendered.] and, in short, everything in the rebellion line has proved unprofitable, and the whole establishment has gone to smash.

FORT WAGNER

But leaving the city behind, which has begun to awaken somewhat to life and in which a large amount of business is still done, we will hire our boat and proceed down the [Charleston] harbor to Fort Wagner. It has changed much since that fatal day [July 18,1863] when [Union] Col. [Robert G.]Shaw led the 54th [Massachusetts Regiment, Colored] to the well-manned ramparts. The mounds and breastworks have washed away; the ditch has been neatly filled up;and but for the old flag-staff and shattered building which mark the spot, it would be confounded by the stranger with the thousand and one mounds of like shape since thrown up in every direction. The New Hampshire and Connecticut men must have attempted to reproduce their old hills, judging by the amount of sand they piled up in different parts of [Morris]Island during that memorable siege!

An old darkey soldier,who was in that great charge and saw the color bearer he was supporting plant the flag on the breastworks and then reel back into the ditch a corpse and who was himself wounded there, accompanied us about the island, imparting much valuable information. He makes his home together with his family in a bomb-proof of [nearby] Battery Gregg and is engaged digging for old iron in the sand. Many a pile he has found and sold. On the day of our visit the products of his industry reminded us of the stacks in a New England hay field. He sells it by the ton and is putting his money in the bank. He described to us how the troops lay behind the "hill yonder" and how they mustered their courage when the New Yorkers said "dem niggers won't fight," and how the shot and shell from Sumter and Gregg killed his file leaders as the column with a yell sprang toward the rebel fort.

Old haversacks, belts, bayonet scabbards, and shoes still strew the ground where the bodies of the fallen were exhumed and taken to Beaufort [South Carolina] for interment in the National Cemetery. [There now lie 9,271 dead,4,513 of them unknown.] But they were not all taken. Ah, no, a sad sight met our eyes when,following our guide, we reached the level sea beach. Human skeletons from which

the sea had washed the sand lay grinning upon the
shore and filled us with sad sensations, which still
haunt our dreams. The sad and the beautiful, how
strangely combined! The same wave that uncovered
their naked bones also brought up the richest and
rarest shells of the great deep [This phrase apparently from Alfred Tennyson's "The Passing of
Arthur," where the line is: "From the great deep
to the great deep he goes."] with which to adorn
them, and all about the skeletons, in the creases
beside their partially imbedded bones, in their
ears, mouth and eyes, the great ocean had deposited her rich gems. As we neared the spot the bones
seemed set in frames of diamonds, which sparkled
and glistened like the rarest gems of India. The
wave too (as if adorning them with the richest of
nature's handiwork was not enough) sang sweet and
melancholy strains as it came slowly up and left a
fillet of snowy foam about the sleepers' heads.
Long we stood and gazed [upon this Gustave Doré-
like tableau]as the sweet waves came and went, reluctantly leaving the heroes farther and farther
upon the beach as the tide receded.

"Who knows," thought we as we lifted a skull and
shook out the shells and said, "but this man was
an acquaintance, a friend, or perhaps a relative?"
[Shakespeare's Hamlet remarked on a similar occasion: "Alas, poor Yorick! I knew him, Horatio."]

Ah, sad, sad thought! They will not always lie
here. For like the human sacrifices of the Aztecs,
they are adorned and favored for a day only to be
crushed when the gods are angry. The very next
wild storm that howls about their shiny sepulchre
will seize them in its chilly arms and carry them
swiftly down to the dark caverns of the treacherous, remorseless sea. Then others will come forth
from the crumbling sand, take their turn with the
ocean decorator, and then follow on to the great
and dread unknown. [Thus recently the bodies of
Colonel Shaw and his Negro troops were washed from
the trench of Fort Wagner into the sea.] As we
looked upon the bodies, the waves, and the high
mounds, we felt the same inspiring sensations which
the traveller feels as he treads the Plains of Marathon [in Greece where, in 490 B.C., the Athenians
defeated the invading Persians].

Here a body of [white-officer-directed]black men,
feeling that perchance this was the only opportu-
nity they would have to win their liberty and assert
their right to freedom, charged upon a superior
enemy and, after a long and terrible battle [in
July 1863] and a siege [from July to September 6],
drove him into the sea. [The Confederate garrison,
the night of September 6, evacuated Forts Wagner
and Gregg and fled in boats.]

"The mountains look on Marathon, and Marathon
looks on the sea." [George Gordon, Lord Byron, *Don Juan.*]

Here, too, is the mound like the one which Grecian guides point out to the traveller and say:
"Here lie the heroes of ancient Athens!" Here, too,
on [nearby] James Island the sea, following the
same old principle, is wearing up to the memorial
mound and soon it, like that at Marathon [and Fort
Wagner], will be swallowed by the greedy waves.
[The poet, Lord] Byron, thought [in his *Childe Harold's Pilgrimage,* canto II, verses 83-92] that the
plains of glorious Greece must inspire every one
with patriotism. So must the mounds of [Fort] Wagner; and no American with a true love of liberty
can walk these shores and not resolve to be more
vigilant and active in the cause of human freedom.
But we forgot, in the enthusiasm that the locality
awakened, that we were sent to describe and not to
moralize. Casting a parting glance at the skeletons and wishing that some clue to their names might
be found, we turned away and walked nearly two miles
to visit the spot on which was erected [on a floating platform in a deep marsh] the "Swamp Angel" [gun
which had been used against Charleston]. But on
nearing the locality we were much disappointed to
find that an arm of the sea now intercepted our
passage.

FORT SUMTER

On returning we launched our boat and in a few
minutes found ourself standing upon the ruined parapet of Fort Sumter [in the harbor of Charleston].
It is nothing but a mound of earth and powdered

brick,almost circular in general outline but very irregular in detail[actually pentagonal]. It shows the marks of many a shot, and the old walls have crumbled to the water's edge, except on the city side,where a few feet of the original wall can be seen. One soldier and his wife occupy a little house on the embankment and have charge of the small wooden light-house erected on the outer side of the fort. One can hardly realize that here[on April 12, 1861] was begun that fratricidal war which swept off our fathers and brothers. The fort is of no consequence now and probably never will be again. [In 1948 it was made a National Monument.] Of [Fort] Moultrie, which is simply an earthwork on Sullivans Island and from which Major [Robert] Anderson escaped to Sumter [December 26,1860], we may write more,but of Castle Pinckney and Fort Ripley,which we visited, we know but little of interest. [Both are in the harbor off Charleston.]

BEAUFORT

Beaufort [pronounced Bú-furt], South Carolina, a watering place [seaside resort for bathing or boating]! Ho! ho! It doesn't look much like it now. Nine years ago it was as fashionable for Southern people to spend their summers here as it is for the wealthy people of the North to go to Saratoga [New York], Long Branch [New Jersey], or Newport [Rhode Island] now! Is that the [Beaufort] beach where the nobility and their ladies used to bathe? Is this the shore along which a hundred pleasure boats were moored? Why, it does not seem possible that this inlet was ever used for anything else but clam-beds. Here, too, you say, they had their outdoor games. In this sand? Whew! No one can travel along here now without sinking into it over his boots. We would as soon think of playing croquet in a meal-barrel.

Then you mean to say that these houses, so dingy and worn,needing so many repairs to make them even comfortable, were once the summer residences of Carolina's proudest sons? That these porches, now decaying and broken,were nine years ago the resort of the pride and beauty of the Sunny South? When

will wonders cease? Why, we should as soon think
of making North End [a Boston slum] a summer resort for Boston, or Five Points [slum district of
lower New York]for the princes of New York,as this
Beaufort of today for the chivalry of the South.
It is the most dusty, dirty, sandy, dingy little
hamlet we ever saw.Its sidewalks are piles of sand;
its palmettoes and live oaks almost shadeless; its
creeks muddy and beachless, lacking the romantic
billow that so often throws cold water upon young
love and young lovers at Gloucester and Province-
town [both Massachusetts resorts]. Its drives are
but other bathing places with waves of sand instead
of water and crests of dust instead of foam; its
finest mansions are empty; and its ballrooms and
music stands are deserted.
   Yet this is Beaufort! There was a time when he
who resided in Beaufort was greater than a king.
[The phrase "greater than a king" Conwell picked
from William Shakespeare's play *Richard II,* IV,1,
1. 305. He used a variation of it ("Yea, there
was a time when to have been a Salemite was greater than a king.") in his travel article, "Battle-
fields of the Revolution," (Boston) *Daily Evening
Traveller,* September 2, 1869, p. 1.] Today a home
here means nothing but poverty,and perchance disgrace. No Southerner who can find a home elsewhere
will live here now. What little business is done
here—and it is mostly confined to retail liquor
establishments and Jewish clothing stores—is done
by men who had never seen the place before the war.
Some few of the old inhabitants remain, but they
are mostly of the class who would have been beside
themselves with joy had Davis, Toombs, Yancey,
Rhett,Memminger, [Alexander] Stephens, or any other
of the "chivalrous nobility"who resided here deigned
at any time to exchange a single word with them.
They and the Negroes affiliate and in some instances
amalgamate—the [Sea]Islands hereabouts being the
only place we found in the South where the whites
and blacks intermarry.
   Yet here,as elsewhere,the omnipotent Yankee may
be found—some who have failed two or three times
and hope soon to be able to fail again. Here reside several of the men who came in the employ of
the Treasury Department and have since remained to

cultivate the Sea Island cotton on plantations they
have purchased. Here, too, are the Yankee school-
ma'ams working as assiduously for the elevation of
the colored race as they did before the arm of the
military was so rudely withdrawn, which promised
the Negroes that all the land in this region should
be their own.

Sadly disappointed when their old masters came
back to take the land, many became completely dis-
couraged and have died from starvation and expo-
sure. Poor men! Knowing full well that there was
no freedom in the South for the poor man any more
than there was for the slave, they had hoped when
[General William] Sherman and [General David] Hunter
told them they were free that the land then appor-
tioned out to them might be left them in peace. But
no, the old rebel slaveholder comes back from his
work of treason; claims his land; [President] Andrew Johnson pardons him; he takes possession; and
the colored man, that in the three years had become
an industrious freeman, sinks into irretrievable
poverty and its consequent slavery. Away in the
sandhills, in the bomb-proofs of forts, under old
forts and decaying tents, this family of colored
men, during the war industrious and happy, are now
passing their lives in the wilderness of the desert islands, along their shores or in the woods of
the inner islands.

Yet we would not be understood as saying that all
the Negroes on the Sea Islands of South Carolina
are wanderers or suffering starvation, for many are
hired by the cotton planters who could not get their
crops without them, and many are cultivating little patches of ground for themselves. One day we
met a Negro fisherman on the shore of [St.] Phillips Island and entered into conversation with him.

"Lor', massa," said he, "I knowed ye mus' come
fum der Norf, caze yer speaks to dis chile. Ise
de man Sam who piloted Genel Sherman when he went
around through de creeks, and Ise aid Genel [Quin-
cy] Gillmore when he dun looked arter de big Fort
[Pulaski] down at Savannah."

"Were you in the army?" asked we.

"Lor, yes. Ise in de fust of dem as what 'listed
ober at Beaufort," said he. "They told us we should
hab land ob our own an den hab houses and cotton

gins,if we'd fust 'list. I 'listed,and here I is.
Who cares a cuss fur old Sam now? Nobody. We cullud folks won't hab nuffin, nor know nuffin, till
dar is annodder mighty oberturning ob der earth."
"What can you expect that will make it better?"
inquired we.
"I dun no! I 'specs you orter know,seein as yer
cums fum der Norf. But I'se may be foolish, yet I
hab a notion like de cullud parson dey hab ober at
der head[Hilton Head Island?]dat de Lord of Glory
will rise up some un ter take care ob dis sufferin
people. I'se no prophet, so I dun know who it'll
be. But he am cummin' shuah! Dat's so!"
The old Negro kicked away at the sand,as he said
this, with a determination which showed his faith
in what he said. The Negroes are not yet out of
the wilderness into which the Lord and their Moses
has led them.
But we are speaking of Beaufort.
Just as we were stepping off the boat at Beaufort,the first man we met was an old army acquaintance, whose face we had not seen since 1864. His
having settled in Beaufort was a fortunate thing
for us. For while we stayed in that vicinity his
house, his horses, his company were always at our
service and made our visit to the Islands of South
Carolina both pleasant and profitable.
He showed us the National Cemetery at Beaufort,
with its shaded walks and white headboards, and
called to our mind when we saw some of these same
men fighting by his side under a flag of the same
texture as the one which now floats over their
graves.[The graves total 9,271 of which only 4,758
are of known servicemen.] He showed us the dilapidated earthworks erected by our forces to protect
the city. [Union troops held the city from Novem-
ber, 1861 until the close of the war.] He pointed out to us the orphan daughters of rebel soldiers
and told their story of wealth and friends before
the war,and of poverty and seclusion since. [He]
showed us the mansion which [secessionist leader
Robert Barnwell] Rhett of South Carolina once occupied and pointed out where Jeff Davis and his family stopped one summer, but the house has since
been burned.

HILTON HEAD

He then accompanied us to Hilton Head [Island], and showed us the falling Fort [Walker], the old house that was used for the post headquarters, the Negro huts made from the old barracks, and explained to us how the fleet of [Flag Officer Samuel F.] duPont sailed around in a circle when the attack was made [November 7, 1861] upon this place and forts [Walker and] Beauregard across the channel. The headland changed much during the week after Sherman['s army] landed there [in December of 1864], becoming a city in those few days, and the change since he left it has been fully as great. It had but few attractions for the soldier even when the island was swarming with troops, and it has decreased since then in beauty and comfort at least 99½ per cent.

ST. PHILLIPS ISLAND

From Hilton Head we went to [St.] Phillips Island, but here, too, nothing but "wild desolation reigned around." [An extension of "Desolation reigned...." in John S.C. Abott, "The March to Atlanta," *The History of the Civil War in America,* vol.2 (New York: Henry Bill, 1866), p. 455.] The forts had partially disappeared; the tents and barracks were gone; and scarce anything was left to remind the visitor of the important event which occurred there. All day we wandered about the islands, admiring the fertility and luxuriant crops of some and wondering at the barrenness of others. How different they appear today from the way they did five years ago when each inlet was full of vessels and on each point a flag; when the sunset guns were heard in every direction, and the drummers' reveille echoed across the waters as the sun arose on the sea.

It was a beautiful evening when we returned to Beaufort and seated ourself on the porch of the hospitable mansion in which our friend resided. The cool breeze from the sea was so delicious and the songs of the birds so sweet that we began to think Beaufort a less dreary place than we had at first supposed. But the sad marks of war were so dis-

tinct and the results of neglect so apparent that
we settled into the conviction the beauty of the
evening was only a faint glimmer that was left of
the glory years ago departed. Our friend came out
and sat beside us, and then in the deepening shadows, within hearing of the Negroes' evening songs
and the patter of the passing steamboats, we sat
and talked of war. It seemed so strange that it
had ever been! Our friend, who was formerly from
Michigan, told us how he came to settle in Beaufort.
Other incidents of the war relating to men we knew
he rehearsed to us until the stars came out and the
lighthouses along the distant coast threw their
flickering light back over the intervening islands.
Then reluctantly saying "good night" to another of
the many army friends we met on our trip, we went
to our couch.

FORT PULASKI

The next day we left Beaufort on a little steamboat that could navigate the shallow creeks and inlets among the islands and had the pleasure before
the sun went down of standing upon the parapet of
Fort Pulaski [near Savannah, Georgia]. The fort
itself [built 1829-47]had been so neatly repaired
by our forces that only here and there the scars
could be seen; but from its walls the remains of
batteries Stanton, Grant, Lyon, Lincoln, Burnside,
Sherman, Halleck, Scott, Sigel, and McClellan, [all]
on [Big] Tybee Island, together with the light-
house and martello tower [round fort topped with
guns] can be distinctly seen [across Tybee Roads].
These, with the works on Bird Island and at Venus
Point, are of special interest for the engineering
skill they display and the remarkable success which
attended the arms behind them. Standing today upon
its walls, and overlooking the scene where the National troops [using rifled cannons for the first
time] performed their herculean tasks, and calling to mind how they managed to transport mortars
weighing eight and a half tons through that soggy,

sloppy swamp, where the mud is 12 feet deep, and did it all under cover of night, one cannot but raise even the highest estimate he has had of both General [Q.A.] Gillmore and his troops for the plan and execution of this almost bloodless battle[April 11, 1862].

It would seem that the expenditure required in repairing this fort [made a National Monument in 1924] was useless, for it has so many times been demonstrated (and especially was it the case here, [April 10-11,1862]) that in these days of [rifled] Parrott guns and iron-clads a stone fort is like some of the land in North Carolina—the more a man has the worse he is off,socially and financially. Much better have no fort than station men behind one of stone or brick to be killed by the [flying] fragments. Stone forts have become merely ornamental now, and the sooner the government takes measures for a better defense of the coast, the less fears we shall have of conflict with maritime nations.

From Fort Pulaski we proceeded up the Savannah River to Savannah. Never have we had a more delightful trip, seen brighter skies or more inviting shores. The river, like the city, is bordered with flowers and trees of every color and variety, the sweet aroma of which fills the air at evening, delighting the senses and invigorating the body.

JACKSONVILLE

We have been in Florida—the fairest land of all the sunny South—that ever-bright peninsula, excelling in natural beauty even the much-praised Italy. We had supposed it to be a much-favored land and credited [that is, believed] nearly all the tales we had heard of its marvelous productiveness,but with all that we were unprepared for the things we saw. The evening when we took our station in a sleeping car at Savannah, the air was chilly and many of our [traveling]companions feared a slight frost, while an overcoat spread upon our bed was by no means uncomfortable. [Maps of 1861-1870 indicate Conwell would have traveled on four railroads by way of Lawton, Georgia, and Live Oak, Florida, junctions.] But when morning came and found

us in Jacksonville [Florida], extra clothing of any
kind was an incumbrance. The sun came out clear
and hot as on a July day in New England, and the
short walk from the depot to the St. James Hotel
brought the perspiration to our face. Yet the heat
was not oppressive. Balmy, clear, and soothing, it
produced none of the debilitated feelings which
come with the warm days of the North.
It was gorgeous, and Nature seemed dressed for a
gala day. Beautiful hedges of hawthorn and cedar
adorned the walks. Trailing vines of bright flowers clung to the trees and arbors. Gardens of roses
representing every hue and shade bordered upon the
streets. Ten thousand lovely blossoms whose names
we cannot recall peeped forth slyly from every nook,
and over all were spread the long evergreen branches of the magnolia, orange, fig, pomegranate, and
pride of India [also called China tree]. Long rows
of cedar, pine, and oak threw out their long arms
over the warehouses and shops along the business
streets, filled by day with birds of every color
and size, and made resonant at night by the whistle
of the whip-poor-will and the song of the nightingale. Enclosing the town we saw luxuriant orchards, said to be apple, pear, peach, cherry and
olive, encircled by green fields of waving grain.
Farther away, and beyond the glittering lakes of
the St. John's River, the pine forests, grand and
silent, stood like a mighty barrier to the progress
of man. As we admiringly gazed upon the scene about
us, a cheerful breeze from the ocean and bright
lakes shook the branches above and around us, filling the air with delicious odor and strewing the
ground with the leaves of a million self-renewing
roses.
It is no wonder to us now that the old and crippled [Spanish explorer Juan] Ponce de Leon should
seek [in 1513] for a [legendary] fountain of perpetual youth between these coral shores. For it
does seem somewhat strange that, in a land where
the blossoms are ever renewed—where the ripe fruit
and the bud hang side by side, and where, if the
harvest is not gathered it proceeds at once to grow
and ripen again, man, God's last creation, should
see but one youth, one manhood, one old age, one
death. Numbers of health seekers, searching for

the same bright bauble which the Spaniard failed to discover, flock here from every State in the Union, hoping to find in the air and climate those healing qualities which De Leon supposed to dwell only in the magic stream of water. Many are healed and go back with health and comparative youth, all through the influence of the climate on disease. The climate did have a curious effect upon this correspondent himself. We alighted in Jacksonville possessed of our usual bodily vigor, but before we had tramped about the streets a single hour we felt so lank, limpsy, and lazy that a vigorous "Reb" could have wrung us out like a rag without eliciting the least objection on our part. Yet it was not that nerveless, sickly sensation which a sudden rise in the thermometer produces at home [back in Massachusetts], but a listless, don't-care feeling akin to the apathy experienced in the last stage of a Turkish bath. Intoxicated with the rich perfume which loaded every breeze, and almost resolved to lie down in the flower beds at some corner and enjoy it, we managed to drag ourselves into the sitting-room of the St. James. There, seating our self sideways into an office-chair, putting our feet on the center table, dropping our arms carelessly over the back of the chair, opening wide our mouth, and shutting our eyes, we proceeded to extract from the wonderful climate a full share of solid pleasure.

As we sat there, drinking in the delicious air with long and deep respirations, we fell into a half doze and dreamed of that other fair and beautiful land, Italy [which we had seen the year before]. Again the leaning tower of Pisa, the colonnades and statues of Florence, the bridges of Venice, the dark Tiber and broken Coliseum of Rome passed before our dreamy vision. Again we mounted our mule and again we quarrelled with the guide, Again we passed the low, dark ruins of Pompeii and the caves of Herculaneum and looked back upon the magnificent bay [of Naples] from the side of [Mount] Vesuvius. Again we went under the dark portal and heard the delightful songs of Southern Italy and were about to repeat those potent words, "See Naples and die" [Mark Twain, *Innocents Abroad,* 1869.],

when we were suddenly snatched from dreamy Italy
to fairer Florida by the falling of our feet from
the table corner and the crash of our hat on the
floor behind us—while the invalid near us coughed
out the sentence, "See Jacksonville and live!"

Some parties, in one corner of the room, were
arranging for a visit to [bandmaster Patrick S.]
Gilmore's [Gilmore wrote words and music of the
popular Civil War song "When Johnny Comes Marching
Home," and was official bandmaster of the Union
Army.] great [National Peace] Jubilee [a spectac-
ular music festival to be held June 15 to 19 in
Boston. See Elie Siegmeister, "Concert Music in
Barnum's Day," *The Music Lover's Handbook* (New
York: William Morrow & Co.,1943), p.738 and 140.].
Others were telling about the crop of bananas,pine-
apples, cocoanuts, dates, figs, quinces, and oranges they were able to cultivate last year, and
one of the party proceeded to show conclusively that
every fifteen acres of orange trees,ten years old,
would bear five million of oranges and clear the
owner $30,000 a year. Another party was telling
how Mr. J. S. Campbell, proprietor of this aptly
named St. James [For St. James's Palace, and the
Court thereof, in London], used to keep on North
Market Street,and afterward in Wilson's Lane,Bos-
ton. [Audrey Kroward, reference librarian of the
Jacksonville Free Public Library, wrote on Novem-
ber 3, 1964, that the proprietor of the hotel in
1869 was Jeremiah R. Campbell,a native of Boston.
The St. James was built during the autumn of 1868
and opened the following New Year's Day. It was a
four-story building with a "French" roof. See also
reference to J.S. Campbell on p.49.] Another enumerated the number of Northern men who have settled in Florida and made out the greater part of
the people of Jacksonville to be from New England.

"This," thought we, "accounts for the handsome
faces and pretty dresses we have seen upon the
streets."

Another,whose lager-beer face and form indicated a foreign birth,was exceedingly perplexed about
the state of the country and remarked incidentally that "Dis gontry ish von grate gontry, but de
troobles pe so much greader as de gontry vich is
so gread as never vas."

The fortifications that surrounded the city [of Jacksonville] are fast washing away, and the "old camp grounds" are either bearing large crops of grain or grown over with vines and small trees. The deserted buildings and open lots where the rebels [in 1863] burned "the Yankee property" are now all occupied by prosperous and enterprising business establishments. Rebel and Federal now live together. Many soldiers who fought here now sell goods to their old enemies or ride a [two-wheeled] velocipede through the streets.

ST. AUGUSTINE

St. Augustine and Fernandina have changed but little since they were garrisoned [in 1862] by the 4th New Hampshire [Regiment, Infantry], except perhaps that the ancient houses and narrow streets of St. Augustine are now covered with a thicker foliage of orange leaves, the trees having grown vigorously during the years that have passed since the war. The national flag still waves over the old [1672-1696] Spanish fort [in 1869 called Fort Marion], and a battery of artillery still garrison there. [Now called Castillo de San Marcos National Monument.]

AROUND SAVANNAH

From Jacksonville we returned to Savannah, the leading city of the South, whose elm and oak shade trees rival New Haven [Connecticut] and whose parks and fountains cannot be excelled by any [other] city in the States for utility and beauty. Here we were shown about the city by a "native Georgian" who took great pains to show us where the Union troops [in 1864] burned whole squares of the city, but who, nevertheless, was like every rebel soldier we have met, genial, kind, and hospitable, leaving nothing undone that could contribute to the pleasure of "a man he had met in the field." Here let us say that wherever we have been abused and cursed as a "d—d Yankee," we always found that the party was a "looker-on" in the rebellion, while those who treated us best were the soldiers who "honorably surrendered."

With this gentleman we made the trip to[nearby] Fort McAllister, with [also] our genial companion Mr. J.[ames?] B. Crocker, Jr.,of [Crocker & Smith Co.?] Boston. But we hardly felt repaid for our long dusty drive when we arrived at the fort near the Ogeechee River and saw only a few low mounds and scattered timbers and nothing by which to identify the spot where General [William B.] Hazen's troops made "the most gallant charge of the war" in full sight of General [William T.] Sherman. The charge on this fort [December 13, 1864] was the grand finale of Sherman's "March to the Sea." Overgrown with trees and surrounded by low, swampy rice fields,it is anything but a pleasant journey which ends at McAllister. [The earthwork fort has been restored approximately to its wartime appearance.] After an hour's search for bastions and magazines, we started [again] for Savannah.

Along the route we saw many detachments of Negroes working in the rice fields,and were informed by our companion that they worked well and were treated well,and our own observation confirms his statement—as well in regard to the Negroes in North and South Carolina as in Georgia. But some of them live like the heathen,and in several fields we saw men and women working together, stark naked, and in many places they wore nothing but an old shirt. A rather questionable way of "keeping cool," we thought,but yet it may be pleasant when people get "used to it." Having occupied so much time at the Fort,it was far in the evening when we arrived in sight of Savannah.

The Negroes had finished their labor, and with the satisfaction of having done an honest day's work,which is the necessary result of free labor, they sat by the roadside singing and chatting in a cheerful and happy manner. At one place we saw a company of well-dressed darkeys gathered around a large fire,which they had built of pine logs, and we were surprised to learn that it was a prayer meeting. We halted a while to listen to their prayers and exhortations,and we must say that many contained more sense, earnestness, and spirit than exhortations in meetings we have attended among the whites.

One old grey-headed darkey spoke nearly as fol-

lows: "Brederen, de goodness of de Lord am spoken about in de Bible, an' when I read him de Lord he spokens to me in dis wise: 'I hab commanded Faro to let my people go, an' I hab led you out of de Egyptian bondage; an' now what? Why, my brederen, we are complainin'. We say de Lord hain't done nuff fur us. We say we want land, we want larnin', but we don't show no ernestness. We many of us won't work wid all our might and get dese things, but complain. Now brederen, we's got to wander in de wilderness forty yeahs an' be most starved and suffer, afore our childern will be purified nuff to go up an' possess de land."
"Amen! Amen! Glory!" came from the whole company after which a sister spoke, and "Old Hundred" ["Doxology"] was sung.

Just before we drove away, an old gentleman got up and said "as how he knowd a Yankee face," that there was "a friend a-listenin' tew de meetin' " (referring to us), and hoped we would bear a "clean record of deir doings to de white brederen of de Norf." At the close of his speech, the whole company, which stared at us and showed us considerable excitement, began a hymn or song to the tune of "Glory Hallelujah," which they sang with such vigor that the dark pine woods echoed back the song from every direction, and we began to fear that some of them would go wild in their efforts to sing louder and the frantic demonstrations they made to show their approval of the sentiment. It almost shocked us, such a sudden transition was it from sacred to temporal things. As near as we can remember, three of the most striking verses ran in this wise, and our memory has been prompted by our friend [Mr. Crocker?], to whom we have shown this [newspaper] copy:

De Yankees am a comin' and de cullud folks is free,
De Yankees am a comin' and de cullud folks is free,
De Yankees am a comin' and de cullud folks is free,
      De Lord am comin' down.

De spirit ob de Lord bress de white folks too,
De spirit ob de Lord bress de white folks too,
De spirit ob de Lord bress de white folks too,
      When de Day ob Judgment comes.

We'll meet Gene'l Butler at de big jubilee,
We'll meet Gene'l Butler at de big jubilee,
We'll meet Gene'l Butler at de big jubilee,
          When we an' he gits dare.

The reference to General Butler evidently dis-
pleased our [Georgia?] companion, who muttered
something about New Orleans,and [we] drove rather
hastily away. Soon after, we were closeted safely
at our hotel, feeling that if the views of Fort
[McAllister] had not repaid our visit, the ideas
gained at the "meeting" had.

UP TO MACON

The next day we made a trip up the [Central]
Railroad into the interior [toward Macon] to look
at the traces of Sherman's great march which are
still to be seen on every side. The whole country
through which he passed [in a three hundred-mile-
long swath of devastation sixty miles wide from
Atlanta to Savannah] is a hideous ruin. Old chimneys, once belonging to the mansions of planters
or the quarters of Negroes, stand surrounded by
weeds and wild shrubs. Old posts and here and there
a broken rail are all that is left of the fences.
The great forests of pine and oak show the ruinous
effects of the fire which followed the sword, and
the Negroes plant cotton between the dead and leaf-
less trees, where before the war was a wild and
impassable thicket. The blackened remains of
bridges, trestle work, and railroad ties are piled
all along the roadside, with here and there a line
of breastworks, and "Jeff Davis neck ties," in the
shape of bars of railroad iron doubled around a
tree, are still to be seen. [How the Southern rail-
ways were thus destroyed is described and pictured
by William Cullen Bryant, Sidney Howard Gay, and
Noah Brooks in "Sherman's March Through Georgia,"
Scribner's Popular History of the United States,
vol. 5 (New York: Charles Scribner's Sons, 1896),
pp. 277-283.]

Dreadful tales the people told us about the march
and said that when for miles and miles around the
sky was red at night with the flames of burning
buildings and forests, and the air was filled with

smoke by day, and when they heard the booming guns and felt the shocks of the heavy pieces, they thought the Day of Judgment had come at last. Many related how the ruthless soldiers came into the parlors and stabled their horses there; how they drove the women and children out of the houses and occupied them as quarters; how they broke up all they could find and then set every building on fire; how they came in the night and awakened the family, politely informing them that their houses and barns were on fire, and leaving them to escape without clothing and in some cases were burned to death; how the soldiers stole or destroyed everything, and the impoverished people were obliged to walk forty miles for a meal to eat—not even a cow, horse, or pig being left; how the men and in some cases the women who attempted to save their buildings or valuables were shot dead at their own thresholds; how the women were ravished and their jewelry and clothes torn from them, and in some instances their hair cut off short and carried away; how the silver handles were torn from the coffin of a corpse that awaited burial and the house set on fire— and many, many tales too sickening and disgusting to be repeated or too hideous to be thought of without chills of horror.

We will not say that we believe all or even one-half the stories they told us. But, alas! the proofs show us some acts of heinous barbarity, preclude a denial, and show the worst side of war. We must say that the ruin and ashes we saw and the tales with which the people filled our head destroyed all the poetry we used to see in [Henry C. Work's Union Army song which ends with the line:] "While we were marching through Georgia."

Surely a blighting curse came upon this people. Slavery was rooted out with fire and its traces washed away in blood. But the cotton and the corn have begun to grow. Here and there a shanty is in process of construction, and soon the same tract of land, under a free-labor system, will "blossom as the rose," and a few years hence war and its horrors will live only in history. Some must die that others may live. Some must suffer that others may be happy.

To-day the ladies of the South have turned out

in vast numbers to decorate the graves of the Confederate dead. Long and gay processions with flags
and carloads of beautiful wreaths move toward the
cemeteries, and the graves are hidden in a forest
of roses. How sad it made us feel to see the long
procession of beautiful women as they filed into
the cemetery at Andersonville(about which we shall
write hereafter), and see them deposit their wreaths
of roses on the graves of the rebel dead for whom
the U.S.Government erected head-boards, after giving them the only shady corner of the cemetery,
while just across the way [about 13,000]graves of
patriots who fought for their nation and were starved
to death for so doing lay naked and barren without
one tribute to show that they [too] left friends
behind. So we plucked some branches of the wild
flowers that grew in the forest and laid the tiny
sprigs upon many a Union grave.

ANDERSONVILLE

Many people have supposed that Andersonville was
a large town. Others, including ourself, supposed
until recently that it was a village of at least
a thousand inhabitants. Nearly every reference we
ever saw made to Andersonville spoke of it in vague
terms—as well they might—or else used the expression "over in the town" and "over in the village" in such a way as to lead the reader to suppose that there was quite a town but a short distance from the stockade. There are many "cities"
in the West and South which exist only on paper,
and Andersonville approaches about as near to a
village as those places do to cities. There are
four or five houses, or rather log shanties, scattered about, in one of which a Georgian keeps a
store and in another of which two ladies from New
England keep a colored school.

The store is established here at this demon-
haunted stockade on the same principle which rules
the grocery establishments that we have seen in
close proximity to many Union cemeteries, and in
some instances many miles from the habitation of
any living human being except the sexton. It seemed
to us in each instance, as if the owner slept Rip-
Van-Winkle-like since the war and only awoke upon

our entrance because the appearance of a customer
was such a novel and unusual occurrence. The meats
in the cellar, the canned fruits on the shelves,
the tobacco and dry goods are, with few exceptions,
such as the soldiers used to buy, and which are
luxuries that the natives cannot afford.
We spoke to a traveling companion [probably another tourist.] about it and expressed our surprise that these groceries should be kept open at
cemeteries where, although there were thousands of
dead, yet there was not a half a dozen living beings that ever saw them. Our friend suggested the
only plausible explanation we have heard by remarking that "these groceries are probably kept
open either out of respect to the memory of the
customers they once had, or, what is more likely,
to keep the field and prevent others from being established there when the millenium comes and all
their old customers come back to trade."
But we will say for the store at Andersonville
that it seemed to have more present customers than
many of the cemetery stores we have seen. For a
cadaverous, long-haired fellow we saw seated on the
steps must be a customer somewhere, if he keeps on
smoking and chewing [tobacco]. As for the transi-
tory trade of the millenium, we do not think the
prospect sufficiently flattering to justify any
investment in the "good will" of the concern. The
cemetery is not a large one, and besides, its occupants went to sleep poor and cannot be expected
to wake up with any large amount of ready cash in
their pockets.
Near by the Andersonville store is the Andersonville Church. Some men who had been prisoners in
the stockade have told us that they never dreamed
that "the old shed over there among the trees"was
a church and never heard of any preaching there.
It must have been the prevailing opinion that it
was a kind of asylum where all the accumulated lunacy of the week was let out on Sunday, *i.e.*, if
the screeching and yelling, which is now heard
there on the Sabbath, was indulged by the [same]
preacher who officiated during the war. Trying to
make up in volume what the sermon lacked in sense,
he screamed away at his hearers as though God were
deaf, and all his auditors—wherever they might be

for miles around—had ears of cast iron.

As for ourself, we have ever since entertained the idea that a face of brass on a head of putty and lungs of steel in a rickety body made a rather poor preacher;and that because a man thinks, himself, that he is doing God's service is no reason at all why he should be permitted to bring reproach upon religion by preaching nonsense from the pulpit in a loud tone of voice. [Conwell himself was ordained a preacher twelve years later and served two churches a total of forty-four years.] Whether the imprisoned soldiers knew it or not, this old church,with its battered seats and tobacco-stained aisles and pulpit, was here when they were here. In it God was requested, in no modest way, to curse the Yankees and to exterminate them from the land.

The Negro school is in one of the old storehouses belonging to the Quartermaster; but where forty scholars come from is a mystery. We asked an old Negro who was working in the field where they all lived, and he could only say, "De Lord knows, I spec; but dis chile only knows dat dey comes."That they come is sufficient encouragement for the self-sacrificing ladies who live there,shunned by every white person and suffering many privations of a more alarming nature. And they work on! If discouragement comes and doubts arise,they have only to look from their window down upon the decaying stockade to be firm again and to feel encouraged in the work which the soldiers began.

The officers' prison pen,near the railroad stopping place—we cannot say station—is the first thing which attracts attention.But its appearance today must be very different from the aspect it presented five years ago [1864-65].Then there was a large rude hut running from one side to another, in which the officers were imprisoned, with the "liberty of the yard," which meant the open space between this hut and the upright row of logs that surrounded it. Then there were sentry boxes on the corners, and guard tents near the gateway. Then there was a crowd of Union officers walking and talking inside, while vigilant [Confederate] sentinels walked without. Now the old rickety hut is gone. The sentry boxes have been torn from the log stockade,and the guard tents are seen no more.

Now there are no more sounds of laughter,of moaning, of sentry challenges, or pastime exercises. For the officers who occupied the stockade,together with the troops that guarded it, have departed. The enclosed space, now that the log hut is removed, is scarcely as large as many country residences.

One cannot realize, as he looks down upon the place from the railroad, that within that solid fence of perpendicular logs [just a few]years ago men suffered for food,for clothing,for water, for medicine, for nursing, for air, and died at last by tens and hundreds for lack of those comforts that were within their sight. One cannot feel down in his heart that such barbarity was ever committed there when he gazes upon it for the first time. Such tales of horror have so much in them, which, although we fully believe the story,yet we cannot feel its truth.

But going from the officers' prison—which was, notwithstanding its privations,a place of comparative comfort—to the "Andersonville Prison" stockade,where the private soldiers were confined, one begins to sense the terrors of prison life. Here the prison pen remains as it was then, with the exception of some decayed logs and the unhinged plank doors.

(At Macon the stockade and everything which could remind [us] of a [military] prison have been removed [prior to 1865] and farmers race their horses on the [Georgia State] Fair grounds without a thought of the dead who died there in 1864. At Millen [Georgia—officially Camp Lawton—through which we passed on route to Andersonville] and Florence [South Carolina, another junction on the rail line between Wilmington and Charleston],some of the stockades remain,but in a dilapidated condition. The land has been cultivated, new buildings constructed, and the army quarters used for fuel,so that even a prisoner who was in Millen for a year said to us that he hardly knew the spot.)

Around this large prison pen [Andersonville—officially Camp Sumter], enclosing 27 acres, still stands the double row of log stockade about 17 feet high. Here and there a log has been undermined by the washing rains and has fallen inward,making an aperture through which a man can squeeze himself. All the guard platforms have been torn down. The wells that were dug on the side hill within the enclosure are fast filling up, and it is dangerous to approach them. The old bakery building on the top of the hill among the trees, and a few rods outside the stockade, is now used as a sheep pen, for which reason all the brick and utensils have been removed.

The hospital barracks are all standing on the south slope of the ravine, although the roof of one has crumbled in and the windows and doors of all have disappeared. The enclosure begins on the side of one hill and running down crosses a slimy brook and extends part way up the hill or slope on the other side. So that within the stockade are two hillsides facing each other across the little marsh through which the water soaks—not runs. At each corner of the stockade, and near the summits of these sloping hills, still stand the redoubts, in which five years ago stood a shining array of rebel cannon, all pointed toward the doomed ones in prison. [About 33,000 men were at one time enclosed there—and the total was nearly 49,500]. The blackberry bushes in the field and forests around grow as luxuriantly as ever; but there are no bony fingers to pick them now, and no hollow voices thanking God for this one little blessing.

The spring about which so much has been written (and which some one said broke out clear as a crystal as a miraculous answer to a prayer then [in August 1864] being offered to the Almighty) is still running, although too filthy, black, and unwholesome to tempt us to drink, as thirsty as we were. ["Providence Spring" was made into a pavilion-covered fountain in 1901.] Several other springs have started out of the ground not many yards from the original one, and the whole side hill seems to be soggy and wet, as if there were numberless springs below. As prisoners have since told us that this was the case when they were confined there, we look upon the breaking out of that spring as a merciful thing in the Providence of God, but in no wise approaching a miracle. If it were so, who prayed for the half dozen springs which have burst through the soil since?

There is no accounting for taste,but if [human-
itarian] Miss [Clara] Barton [Sundial Monument
commemorates her work in identifying the Union dead
at Andersonville and marking their graves in 1865.]
drank from this dark and green stream of water,and
was so infatuated with the romance of the thing to
call it "clear and cool," her organs of taste must
be less sensitive than ours and her eyes less clear.
The water has at present an unpleasant odor,a very
brackish taste, and a disgusting appearance. When
we take into consideration that this was sweet and
clear to the soldiers in comparison to that which
they had been drinking, we say, Lord deliver us
from the other beverage. But a few feet from this
spring is the stream of water from which the soldiers did drink when the wells failed and no spring
was known. Now there are no soldiers to roil it
beyond the stockade;no mules, horses, or cattle to
lie in it;no guards to maliciously taint its water
with offal and decayed animal substances.Yet now,
in the absence of all this, the pool which soaks
along through the weeds and grass emits a very offensive odor and is covered with a green-and-yel-
low scum that shows the rankest poisons of earth
and air. Over the whole area has sprung up a rank
growth of weeds and canes, among which the flocks
of sheep now obtain a scanty sustenance,and through
which the fox and rabbit skip at the approach of
human feet.
    Amid solitary and wild surroundings, almost en-
circled by a forest of tall pines, and all its
camps deserted, the ruins of Andersonville Prison
remain to force upon the visitor's memory all the
fearful pictures of the past. Enough remains to
serve as a strong link between the present and the
past, and all that series of horrors which has
blackened the history of this civilized people
comes up with them. We had thought of giving its
history somewhat in detail and had written how we
felt as we recalled it when standing on the spot;
but oh! it is harrowing enough to think of the
filth, the stench, the heat, the thirst, the hun-
ger, the worm-filled food, the fever, the ague,the
scurvy, and to hear about the gangrenous cancers,
running sores, and vermin-eaten limbs, and of the
filthy bread and still more nasty water; and then

to imagine how the[prisoners]raved in their thirsty lunacy or how the hollow laughter of the hunger-made idiots chilled the blood of their bed-ridden comrades.Oh! yes,it is enough to mention it without exciting the anger of the patriotic or racking the sensitive nerves of the sympathizing with a detailed description. It has passed into history, and by the disinterested has been partially forgotten.

To call it all to mind again,with the additional hideousness in which it appears in the light of recently discovered facts would be only to widen the breach between the "brethren of the two sections" and make the demand for hangman's hemp so great as to conflict seriously with the present movements towards a "permanent peace." Politicians and civilians,and perchance statesmen, may forget such wrongs in their desire for temporal gain,but the soldier who suffers or the widow who mourns cannot forget. The soldiers of the Republic are generousness enough to forgive those who conspired against the nation,and forgiving enough to welcome as a friend any of the brave men they met in the field who fought as if they believed in the cause they represented. But never can the Union soldiers be so inhuman, so cowardly and vile as to fraternize, or treat otherwise than as criminals, the men who tortured, starved,and murdered[more than] 12,000 of their bravest comrades in the vermin-breeding dens of Andersonville Prison. [The area is now a state park. For an earlier description of Andersonville,see John T. Trowbridge's (edited by Gordon Carroll) *The Desolate South 1865-1866* (New York: Duell, Sloan, & Pearce, 1956), pp.247-252.]

With such thoughts disturbing our peace of mind, we waded through the dry weeds which now cover the hard beds of soldiers or hide from view the spots where like swine they wallowed, and then left the stockade to visit the [National] Cemetery [Officially established July 26, 1865.]. In an open spot, a short distance to the northeast of the prison-pen, the last remains of the murdered ones lie sleeping their last sleep. Side by side the [more than] 12,500 now rest, while over them wave the Stars and Stripes of the nation for which they died. Simple graves! A little sandy mound, a white headboard bearing the name—and the whole story of their resting place is told. When we neared the gate through which the visitor must pass the high board fence which surrounds the cemetery, we were surprised to see quite a large party of ladies and gentlemen in the cemetery under the shade of the trees throwing flowers upon the graves. While we were standing by the flagstaff and contemplating their movements, another party entered the gateway, and passing near us, walked on toward the other company. Just as they passed us a lady dressed in the richest attire and possessing really handsome features stepped a little way from her companions and with gestures indicating the deepest disgust, scornfully spat upon the grave of a Michigan soldier. Down in the forest we found a large variety of wild flowers. Beside every tree and under the hanging edge of rocks they bloomed in beauty and filled the air with delicious perfume. From these we selected the varieties which pleased us most, and with an armful returned to the cemetery and laid them one by one upon the graves.

On our return to Macon we met an ex-Confederate soldier who had been a guard at Andersonville and Millen. He was quite sociable and communicative, especially on the subject of military prisons.

"I have stood guard many a night," said he, "when the nights were freezing and the day scorching, wishing I had better quarters. But mine were palaces beside the awnings under which the Federal prisoners slept."

MONTGOMERY

God bless the man that invented diaries! They are the only preventatives now in use to keep wandering correspondents from insanity. Even with them, we feel as if life was only a "lucid interval" [John Dryden, "Mac Flecknoe."], so strangely and inconsistently are the evils and virtues, pleasures and pains of life jumbled together in the experience of a Northern man who visits and observes the people of the South. Now for the diary!

While we were making arrangements to pass the night (we cannot say sleep) in the sleeping car [Patented 1864 and 1865 by George M. Pullman.] which carried us from Macon to Montgomery, Alabama, and just as we had begun to wish for a better bed, the cars [of the South Western & Muscagee Railroad] stopped at a small station, and a blushing couple, "hold of hands," came into the car. Their appearance as they stood hesitatingly in the door-way showed that they meant "mischief" [William Shakespeare, *Hamlet* : "...it means mischief."] and were just starting out on their wedding tour.

"Would you like a berth, sir?" said the lively, jolly-faced conductor of the miserable sleeping car.

"No, sir—I recon—as mat be—that ain't what we want," stammered the bridegroom. "Haint you got no bridal chamber on this ere kear?"

"Oh, the bridal chamber!" exclaimed the conductor. "Come this way, sir."

The couple went tremblingly through the car to the "state room" which looked about as much like a state room on a Northern sleeping-car as a cell in the county jail appears like the Parker House [a Boston hotel] parlor.

"Does that door shut up?" anxiously inquired the bridegroom.

"Oh, yes. See how it slides," said the conductor.

"But I'm dogged if I see any place to sleep," suggested the applicant for the chamber.

"Oh, we'll fix that, if you will be seated," said the conductor, pointing to a low, hard sofa on the opposite side of the car, close to the head of our curtained couch.

"I don't like it; so there!" whispered the bride.

"Don't like what?" said her partner.

"I won't go no farther, I won't, if you keep talking so."

"What have I done, I'd like ter know?"

"You told him you didn't see no place to sleep, and I don't think it was usin' me right."

"Well, I don't see no place now, neither. If we've got to be tucked away in that little hole, we'll haft ter stan' up all night, that's sartin."

"Let's go back, Johnny; I'm afraid to go any further."

"Oh, no, let's don't go back. Let's stick er eout."

"I can't. I won't, I don't like ter. I can't
stay here. Theer lots of men behind those cur-
tains. I'm sick. I won't go no farther. Say,
Johnny,let's do go home. Do,I want ter so much."
And the fair one began to weep as though her heart
would break.
"Wall,don't cry,Mollie, we'll git right eout at
the next place. But you hadn't orter be so 'fraid
o' folks, now we're married."
This seemed to quiet her grief, and at the next
station the afflicted couple left the cars,having
paid for the "state room," and we heard him,as he
stood on the platform outside, remark, "That ar
sleepin' kear was doggoned small quarters for married folks."
In the morning, before the arrival of the train
at Montgomery, we arose from our sleepless couch
and seated ourselves with a large fat man whose
rest, like ours,had been anything but refreshing.
He was,however,in a very agreeable state of mind,
and upon learning that we were from Massachusetts,
engaged earnestly in conversation. We soon learned
that he was a Presbyterian minister and owned a
large plantation in Georgia. He stated that he
lived in Oglethorpe,near Andersonville,and he was
a chaplain during the war. He related many incidents of war life and said that he met a Massachusetts chaplain in the prisoners' camp,who,one day
while they were hauling wood, suddenly got angry
at the mule and cursed terribly.And when the speaker reproved him for the sin the profaner excused
himself by saying that he was on "indefinite leave
of absence from God and God's people."
He stated that he often visited the sick prisoners and that there were many Massachusetts men
buried at Harper's Ferry and vicinity whose names
we could get and whose graves we could find on ap-
plication to a gentleman to whom he would give us
a letter of introduction. He stated incidentally
that the Massachusetts cavalry around Winchester,
and in fact all who were stationed there, were as
near "devils" as men could well be.
"Why," said he, "they had no more fear of death
than a brute."
After a time the conversation turned upon politics and the state of the South.

"What do you think of the war?" asked we. "Do you see in it the hand of God?"

"No, sir, not at all. The devil and the Yankees produced that awful disaster."

"Don't you,as a Presbyterian,believe that God's hand is connected with all the changes and events of life?"

"Well, I can't exactly say; I cannot see how— no,no,sir;the devil conducted the affairs of the late war, aided by his satellites, the Yankees."

"I am a little surprised at your doctrine,for I cannot but believe that God permitted this bloodshed in order that many things might be accomplished,and one of these things was the extinction of slavery."

"Ha! ha! ha! ho! ho!" laughed he, "is that your doctrine? That is the most damnable and inconsistent doctrine ever suggested! Why,the niggers were better off in every particular;had more pleasure, more money, were better members of the community as slaves, and God decreed that they should be slaves, and when the Yankees freed them they [the Yankees] ignored the Bible and a curse is now coming upon them."

"What curse?"

"The race is running out. Talk about educating the nigger! when the civilization you have in the North is cursed of God. The women of the civilized Yankee don't have children, and the race of the Yankee and the nigger is doomed together. The niggers have but few children now, and fifty years hence there will be but few left to quarrel over. Their doom is sealed when you attempt to civilize them. You Yankees don't know what you are about. But when your cotton mills all come to Georgia and Alabama, when all that's left for you to do is to furnish the world with ice and stone, then maybe you will begin to see the effect on the North of this abolitionism."

"Don't you regard it as a religious duty to educate the people?" asked we.

"No, sir. The Jews were the most favored people on earth,and not more than one in fifty could read or write. It is convenient but not a duty."

"Did you own slaves yourself?" again we asked.

"Yes, sir; forty of them. One day [in April,

1865] I stripped a dozen of them and thrashed them for not attending church, as was my duty, and the next day [the cavalry of General James H.] Wilson made a raid on us, freeing the whole lot, and now I never see one of them niggers without his threatening to thrash me. Now I didn't lash them because I loved to do so, simply,but as a matter of duty, for I was responsible for their religious welfare."

"Your view of the matter surprises me somewhat, considering your profession," said we. "When the Yankees came down here to restore the Union, they did not think of freeing the slaves."

"O! you cannot make me believe that. The Yankees calculated on the chances. They saw they had the inside track,and to vent their spite,they sent men down to fight. The Yankees didn't come themselves;they hired Germans and Irishmen to do their fighting for them, while they lived at ease and made money. The Yankee has overpowered us—not conquered us—and now I suppose the devil will be "loose for a thousand years"[See Revelation 20:2.].

The arrival of the [Montgomery & West Point Railroad] train at Montgomery closed the conversation, and we insert it here as it is merely a rehearsal of the same ideas that we have heard in a hundred other places since our wanderings began. The [people of the] South now see how foolish and ill-advised was their rebellion,but the animus [hostile spirit] of the war still remains. Northern men in the South are everywhere treated with respect,and for ourself,we can say,with hospitality and kindness. But it is the influence of Northern capital, and not of fraternal feeling, which induces the people to behave as they do. Those who served in the Confederate army, however, are universally genial in their intercourse with the soldiers of the North,and in many places have we been made the recipient of kind attentions merely because we "were a soldier."

But in many cases the respect the soldiers have shown us has been cancelled by the mean and slanderous attacks the press has made upon us. Our letters have been clipped, hacked,and interlined, and in some cases paragraphs original with the contemptible editor himself have been quoted as coming from the [Daily Evening] Traveller and being written by us, in which the vilest spirit of Copperheadism gleams out of every word. In a few weeks we hope to feel competent to write an article showing, as far as a Northern man can see, the present state of the South. Reconstruction on a new and higher basis is fast being accomplished, and the South is destined to become a rich and populous country. Those merchants of New York and Boston who now introduce themselves to the Southern trade will be, before many years, the richest men of the land. Now is their only chançe. Months hence it will be too late. For the tide must turn, and if it flow not northward it will flow Europeward.

Upon our arrival in Montgomery, ["The Cradle of the Confederacy"], we took up our abode in the Exchange Hotel, from the balcony of which Jeff Davis [of Mississippi] made his great speech before his inauguration [at the Capitol on February 18] in 1861 [as president of the Confederate provisional government]. [He was introduced by Alabama lawyer William L. Yancey with the words, "The man and the hour have met." A plaque commemorates the event.] The appearance of the city hardly fulfils our expectations, as there are but few fine residences or blocks, and all the business seems to be confined pretty much to one square. We had heard so little before and have known so little since the time of the Secession Convention which elected Jeff Davis president of the Confederacy, that all our impressions in regard to the city have been gained from descriptions given then.

We feel that in order to see the Montgomery which our imagination painted for us we must see the throngs of people—the long lines of infantry with gay uniforms, and torches on their bayonets—the crowds of fine ladies dressed in Confederate colors and wearing secession bonnets. The great boulevard, with the State House at the upper end and the Exchange Hotel at the other, jammed with fiery Southerners shouting and cheering for the Confederacy and Davis; the windows, doors, and balconies of the dwellings decorated with secession flags and traitorous devices [that is, emblems and mottos]; the rows of shade trees filled with banners in the day and illuminations by night; the grand old State House on the hill, filled with conspirators; [the original] Exchange Hotel [the center of political and social life] overrun with visitors from other cities. We feel a sense of disappointment that Davis does not appear on the balcony and shout to the crowd: "The North shall smell Southern powder, and feel Southern steel!" Where is [secessionist Robert B.] Rhett, who wished the North to let him alone, and the convention to give him the presidency? Where are [Confederate statesman] Howell Cobb, [General Louis] Wigfall, [Robert] Toombs, [LeRoy] Walker, [John] Perkins, [Alexander H.] Stephens, [Robert W.] Barnwell, and [Lawrence] Keitt? Where are the conspirators who stood around Davis when, from the platform in front of the State House [spot now marked by a bronze star.], he gave his inaugural address, and urged "retaliation on the commerce of the enemy"? Where are the editors whose mighty pens spurred on the Hydra of Rebellion?

It is useless to make inquiry, for the appearance of the city furnishes an answer too full for comment. Aladdin lost his lamp and the scene changed. The Montgomery of to-day [1869] and the Montgomery of 1861 are most singularly in contrast. The two Negroes who, as slaves, stood beside Jefferson Davis, holding candles that he might see to read his incendiary speech, to-day, as freemen, hold offices of trust and profit. The ladies who then left their black servants at home to cook and wash, while they exhibited themselves on the streets in the "red and white" of treason, now daub their own fingers with dough and make up their old dresses with their own hands for their pallid and frail little girls.

The newspaper [Montgomery *Advertiser*?] which then contained the following, "Let them come down and fight; two or even three to one, and we will whip them back to their very thresholds," to-day has an article beginning: "The Ladies' Memorial Association yesterday observed the anniversary of The Lost Cause by floral offerings upon the graves of those Southern patriots who fell in defence of the American Constitution."

The crowd of people who then pressed up the wide street toward the Capitol, until women fainted and men yelled for a chance to breathe, are now in the country holding the plough or sitting on the corners and cursing the nigger. The gay ranks of soldiers who went to the war with the idea that all it needed was a "dress parade" to make the Yankees skedaddle, now sleep under those long rows of mounds in yonder cemetery. The flagstaff on the Capitol, which on the 4th of March, 1861, bore the [Stars and Bars] flag of the Confederacy, then unfurled for the first time, has given place to a shorter one on which the Stars and Stripes now wave in silent majesty.

The cotton warehouses, which occupied whole squares of the city, have since been burned by the "Confederate authorities" to prevent their contents from falling into the hands of [General] Wilson's raiders, and to-day the tall ruins mock them for their incendiarism. Behind the counters where then the sprigs of Southern chivalry dealt out ribbons or pills, to-day the Northern "mudsill" trades in cottons, provisions, or drugs.

The elegant church [the First Baptist of Montgomery] which then gave up its vestry [room] that the blacks might occupy it for worship is now [in 1869] silent and empty, and its owners have made practical the theory expressed in their church resolutions that "no Radical [Reconstruction Republican] can worship our God." The Negroes, who in simple faith tried to worship then in that vestry, have since [1866] been provided with a church by a "Baptist radical" and are permitted to meet together undisturbed in their own building [the Columbus Street Baptist Church].

[Milo B. Howard, Jr., assistant director of the State Department of Archives and History at Montgomery, explained in a letter written January 10, 1967 to the editor of this book: "The Negro Baptists belonged to the same Baptist church as the white people, and in fact outnumbered the white members. This church was known as the First Baptist Church of Montgomery and was [at] Madison Avenue and North Court Street. In 1866 some Baptist missionaries, fearing that the white people were taking advantage of the Negroes, formed a Baptist church known then as the Columbus Street Baptist Church because it was [at] Columbus Street and Ripley Street. This congregation is still in existence and is known as the First Baptist Church (Negro)."]

A lady who then was worth a hundred thousand dollars—who lived in fine style then, but who has since lost her husband in the war and her property by fire and raids—to-day wanders about the streets, begging for a piece of bread to eat. She told your correspondent, as she stood on the Capitol steps, "Here my husband was honored where I am now a beggar." All was gay then that is solemn now. The slave then is a legislator now; uproar and confusion then where all is quiet now; then war and rebellion, now peace and loyalty.

Before we left the city we went in search of a [former] brigadier general, who was in the Confederate service, and to whom we procured letters of introduction. We found the grave official [General Braxton Bragg—omission of the name in the *Traveller* probably was a typesetter's error. Bragg between 1865 and 1869 was chief civil engineer of Alabama. His residence in 1869 (when he was 52) was in Mobile, where he had suprvised harbor improvements, and he must have boarded and lodged in Montgomery when at the capital on official business. Don C. Seitz's biography, *Braxton Bragg: General of the Confederacy* (Columbia, South Carolina: The State Co., 1924) says that just before Bragg died unexpectedly, in 1876, he "appeared to be in his usual grave but cheerful humor."] sitting on a bale of cotton, swinging his feet and rapping a board with his knuckles, keeping time to the song:

> I wish I was a geese,
> Caise then I'd live in peace,
> An' gedder up much grease,
> Eatin' corn, eatin' corn.

[These lines suggest G.W. Hunt's 1869 comic ballad "I Wish I Was a Fish." However, Conwell (and likewise Bragg) remembered them that way from the doleful four-stanza song "Over There," whose third stanza actually goes:

> "Oh! I wish I was a geese
>   All forlorn!
> Oh! I wish I was a geese
>   All forlorn!

> Oh! I wish I was a geese,
> 'Cause they lives and dies in peace,
> And accumulates much grease
> Eating corn!"

Complete words and music appear in *The Diamond Collection of Songs,* H. Franklin Jones (Brooklyn, April, 1895), p. 254. Reportedly it was authored by a person named Hutchinson, and first published in 1844 by J.F. Atwill of New York. The silly ditty (with a commentary) also is found in Sigmund Spaeth's book *Read 'Em and Weep* (New York: Arco Publishing Company, 1945), pp.30-31. Oliver Ditson,of Boston, published an edition of its sheet music in 1857.]

He appeared glad to see us, however, and after reading our letters [of introduction] invited us to his boarding house, where he kept his diary of events. Unfortunately he could not find it in time to show us before we felt obliged to leave,in order to take the evening train for Mobile.

MOBILE

When we were at Mobile, Alabama, searching for the lines of earthworks which were erected at the time it was besieged [1864 and 1865], we fell in with a dirty specimen of the "poor whites" of the South who seemed to think it an honor to be acquainted with a newspaper correspondent. He followed us wherever we went,scrutinizing every movement we made and exclaiming every few moments, "What on airth ar yer looking arter forts and things for which have long since been dug away?"

In spite of all our endeavors to make him believe that all the purpose we had in wandering over these fields was to find where a fort had been,he still claimed the privilege of doubting our word.

"Now, look 'e here, stranger," exclaimed he, "you are a Yankee,and them's mighty smart fellers. And I know that no Yankee o' your size would be foolin' round in those bushes without he was arter sunthin'. Yer may laugh, stranger, but yer can't feule me. Yer arter Captain Kidd's money,and I'll bet the licker yer know where it is."

We though at first that he was trying to "fool" us and regarded it as a huge burlesque. But we became convinced, after a lengthy conversation, that he was in earnest and really believed that we were searching for the hidden treasures which, according to tradition, the [British privateer and] pirate Captain [William] Kidd "buried somewhere."In this conversation we learned that a circle of enthusiasts, believing that the hiding place of the treasure would be revealed to them by pronouncing over it certain potent words given to one of their number in a vision, had been searching the fields and forests for twenty miles around Mobile for the evidences which were said to mark the spot.

The excitement in Mobile had been considerable, and the spiritualists and clairvoyants had been consulted in regard to it.The spiritualists claimed that Kidd's treasure had been washed into the sea, and the clairvoyants, that it was covered a hundred feet by sand. This discouraging view of the case from such high authorities did not deter the members of the "charmed circle" from prosecuting the search, of which our persevering follower was a member. Oh, he was sure it was hereabouts, and they were sure to find it if no Yankee got ahead of them, and they were going to dig that night. All our endeavors to persuade him to let us accompany him were fruitless, as he dared not break his "holy compact," as he called it.

We had heard so many stories about the search for this treasure in our younger days that we felt at once a lively interest in the enterprise. Thinking of the usual charm used in such extremities, we offered him a $5 greenback to take us with him; and much to our surprise he acceded to the proposition, with the proviso that we were to have none of the [Kidd] money and that the consent of his companions should first be gotten. Leaving him to find the other members of the "charmed circle" and get their consent, we went to our hotel to get tea and wait for his arrival. At about eleven o'clock P.M. he came, with another as disagreeable-appearing man as himself, and, with a smiling face, informed us that we could go with them. Before we went out, however, he said to us slyly that he did not wish his companions to know that we gave him any money.

Out into the darkness we went with these strange men, feeling the liveliest interest in something,

we knew not what. It was an adventure, and that
was all we cared. Here was an "item" [A possible
newspaper story or feature article.]and woe be to
the correspondent who would not venture something
to get it. At a corner of the Park we found several other men waiting who whispered for a few minutes to our companions and then led the way through
by-streets and alleys into the low, marshy fields
that border upon the [Mobile] river or inlet [Mo-
bile Bay]. Here they stopped and discussed their
plans,and gave us to understand that after one of
the party said "Auburn," not a word was to be spok-
en by any one unless "something spoke to them."
What this something might be we did not inquire,as
we were only a passenger,and had only to do as we
were bid.

It was too dark for us to make out the features
of any of the party, but we saw that a lank tall
man, with a high beaver hat, was the leader, and
the facility with which he strode over the marshes
and mud holes that partially engulphed the rest of
the party was truly surprising. All the way,which
led through the brush and over the ploughed fields,
we felt very much as if we would like to lie down
on the damp sward and have one hearty laugh. But
our interest in the occasion was somewhat increased
by hearing the magic word, "Auburn," and seeing a
sudden stop,with various awkward motions,in which
the whole party joined. They had reached the
charmed spot!

One man took us by the arm and silently pointed
to the ground,as much as to say "Sit down,"and we
at once seated ourself in the dew-saturated grass.
It was quite dark, but by straining our eyes we
were able to make out the greater part of their motions. Two stood near us, making gestures with
their hands,very much like the motions made by
signal men in the army;two others,"hold of hands,"
made motions like those we have seen little girls
make when playing "Wash the Ladies' Dishes."

The tall man with a spade began to dig away with
all his might, taking little care in his hurry
whether he buried us or not,provided he found the
treasure. For a long time we sat there watching
their ceaseless motion,while the spade grated into
the gravel and the breath of the digger began to

come hard. Suddenly he ceased to throw out the dirt and began to strike his spade into the ground with all his strength. The fire flew from its bright edge as it collided with the gravel-stones, while the dull "chunk-chunk" sound showed that something more flexible than stone or dirt had been reached by the enthusiast. We began to believe that he had found the treasure, as he shoveled off the gravel and struck upon what was evidently partially rotted wood. We could scarcely restrain ourself from rising and rushing to the spot and began to think how foolish we were to forego our claim for a share in the treasure for the paltry sum of five dollars. The others evidently shared in our excitement, but with commendable perseverance kept on with their queer motions.

Crack! crack! up came a piece of wood, and away it went into the field from the excited hand of the digger. Crack! and up came another. This time the motions of the party around almost ceased as they excitedly stretched their heads toward the hole. For a full half hour the tall man with the spade worked on, bringing up splinter after splinter of wood from the apparently inexhaustible bed, until at last it utterly refused to come out at his command. He then laid aside his spade and began to throw out the dirt and pull up pieces of wood with his hands until at last even this failed him, and his work was evidently at a standstill. For a few moments he stood puzzling himself as to what he should do, while his comrades kept working vigorously at their "charming motions."

We had become fully persuaded that the treasure was there, when he suddenly made several motions with his hands over the place and, taking his spade, beckoned the company to follow him. After the company, with ourself tagging on behind, had left the place about a half a mile, the tall man stopped and, taking off his hat to wipe his forehead, said: "Fellers, this is far enough away now, and I'll tell yer. I struck on a d—d old log that is as tough as linktun vity [that is, lignum vitae]. But I be gummed ef I don't believe that ther money is thereabouts somewhere."

Many a profane word gave notice of his comrades' disappointment at this piece of information, and

several were for getting axes and going right back.
But when the tall man told them that the "vision
said between twelve and one" they all started toward the city. As for ourselves, tired, wet, and
sore, we were glad we did not pay but $5 for the
privilege of being made a dupe of the superstition
of others. At the outskirts of the city the company parted with many cautions "to tell nobody and
be on hand tomorrow night,"and we went to our hotel to dream of the treasures which the pirate
buried. Whether they went the next night, we do
not know, as we left the city the next day. We
think now that taking part in the search for Captain Kidd's treasure was the most foolish expenditure of time,strength,and money that we ever made.

NEW ORLEANS

On a floating marsh that is said to be gradually
sinking under its load stands the great commercial
city of New Orleans. Full of life, every street
crowded,and covered with the foliage and blossoms
of beautiful magnolias and orange trees,it may be
said to be the most beautiful city in North America. There are many things in and about it to remind one of French cities and to justify the claim
of its inhabitants that it is "a second Paris."
Beautiful city! Wide avenues, shady walks, grand
old buildings,lovely drives,cooling fruit groves,
clear sunshine! The spectator of to-day,who notes
the prosperous streets, the crowded markets, and
loaded wharves,can hardly realize that these same
streets have been the arena of so many terrible
combats or the stage upon which so many fearful
tragedies and important comedies have been acted.

Canal Street today,with its decorated show windows,clean pavements, and trains of street cars,
has a very different appearance from the spectacle
seen there on that other first of May [1862] when
the 31st Massachusetts [the first Union Regiment
to enter the city]and the Fourth Wisconsin Infantry,
with Captain [Charles] Everett's [6th Battery,
Massachusetts Light] Artillery, marched along the
street, escorting General [Benjamin F.] Butler
through the surging mob to the St. Charles Hotel.
The levee has a very different aspect from that it

presented to [Admiral David G.] Farragut's [con-
quering] fleet [April 25,1862] as he moored alongside blazing warehouses, smoking ruins of shipping, and the smouldering heaps of cotton. The
people that appear [now,in 1869] on the sidewalks
with their gold-headed canes,poodle dogs,and jewelry have a softer, less offensive look than the
bare-headed,grizzly rabble that welcomed the Yankees[seven years ago]with threats and imprecations.
The dark, deep [Mississippi] river that threatens
each spring to overflow its [levee-protected]banks
and come down into the [lowlands] basin occupied
by the city bears to and fro a hundred steamboats
where drifted then the frowning flagship or threatening gunboat.

[Conwell does not state clearly how he traveled
from Mobile to New Orleans. Three transportation
means were possible: (1) coastal steamer through
Mississippi Sound, three years earlier, another
reporter traveled *eastward* from New Orleans to Mobile by steamer. See Trowbridge, p. 216-217; (2)
A group of rail lines with changes at Meridian and
Jackson in Mississippi; (3) the New Orleans, Mobile & Texas Railroad. He only comments ambigu-
ously:]

When we left the train which brought us from Lake
Pontchartrain we almost expected to see the same
men and witness the same scenes which occurred in
1862. We well knew they would not be there; but
all our previous ideas of the city had been so in-
terwoven with thoughts of insurrections, mobs,and
battles that the simple mention of the name called
up the scenes of war. Then the streets, the old
Custom House,the statues of [General Andrew]Jack-
son [the city's defender in 1815] and [statesman
Henry] Clay,the Saint Charles Hotel,and the crowded markets all serve as a connecting link between
the present and the past.

One needs only to walk up St.Charles or Poydras
Street and see the handsome faces that adorn the
latticed windows or the beautiful forms that grace
the sidewalk to be reminded of that army of ladies
who, pistol in hand, rushed through the streets
crying, "Burn the town! Destroy the city! Don't
mind us!" Beautiful dolls in times of peace, almost indispensible as parlor ornaments in time of

prosperity, but rather poor material for fighting in time of war. We have never heard that a single one of this host of armed Amazons ever mastered sufficient courage to discharge a revolver. But they were a power then. From street to street and house to house, they ran with dishevelled hair and flushed faces, stirring up the spirit of chivalry and rebellion. But the horrid men wouldn't come up to the scratch. The "fellers" had seen too many artifically red faces and too many tousled curls draggling down the ladies' backs before, to be stirred by them to deeds of valor in the presence of Farragut's fleet and the corps of foreigners. So the dishevelled-haired, red-faced dodge became a failure, and the sweet dears went home to comb their hair and fix up to receive the Yankees.

The next day the Yankees came. The city was hid in a huge cloud of smoke. Buildings were burning; women were flying to the country; and Canal Street and the levee were packed by a furious uncontrollable crowd of "plug-uglies," whose occupation had been gambling and fighting and whose present desire was to murder and assassinate. From the great ships came the blue uniforms, the bright bayonets, and pavement-shaking artillery, and forming on the wharf, pierced the crowd and wound up Poydras and St. Charles Streets to the [St. Charles] Hotel.

General Butler was there, marching coolly along between a file of soldiers, the object of everybody's attention. Brave man! a general in battle has the excitement of the rattle, the yells, the booming, and the smoke to lift his courage and take his thoughts from personal danger. But he who can deliberately, without hesitation or fear, march through an army of infuriated roughs that is seeking for any little chance to shoot or stab him, with his sword in his sheath and his revolver in his belt, can be none other than a constitutionally brave man. He that could sit unconcernedly in his room while the mob were crying for his head without and while his best defenders gave up the city for lost and could order the artillery to open on a crowd of a hundred times the number of the garrison without a doubt as to its result is something more than an ordinary man. General Butler may have made some mistakes in his life, but his behavior at New Orleans [as military governor in 1862] is surely not one of them. General Butler is gone [from that city now] and the mob that threatened him are gone. But, as in almost every other instance, the General has outlived his enemies and their machinations to injure him.

Into the uncompleted Custom House, upon which General [Pierre G.T.] Beauregard was working when he abandoned architecture for the field, we went, admiring the grand design and the ponderous masonry of the building. In the rooms where the troops were quartered during the war we found the desks of busy clerks surrounded by piles of official papers and bundles of red tape. In the basement was the Post Office, occupying nearly the whole floor, and its entrance filled at all hours of the day with an anxious-faced crowd.

On the second floor, the way to which is up the same old rickety plank stairs, is the room occupied by General [James] Longstreet [then in the insurance and cotton-factor businesses]. He was there when we went in and greeted us in a very cordial manner. He hoped the war was over and prayed for peace. We told him we thought his prayers would be answered and then left to make a call on General [John B.] Hood.

We found him running a one-horse commission store on the second floor of a stone building on a side street. He was very sociable and talked freely about the war, and said he regretted nothing he had done, and would do the same fighting over again if he had a chance. He said when he succeeded General [Joseph E.] Johnston [in 1864] in command of the Western [Department of the] Confederate Army he knew the game was up. He was only fighting to save his honor. The "revolution" was crushed when Vicksburg fell, and he said so at the time. He said it was painful for him to talk about The Lost Cause and he did not like to recall the war. He arose on his crutches [He had been minus a leg since the Battle of Chickamauga.] when we left, bidding us goodbye with an emphasis which indicated that he would like to have us call again; so we have kept a good opinion of General Hood.

General Beauregard received our formal call in that dignified manner which all men who have "had greatness thrust upon them" [William Shakespeare, *Twelfth Night*, II, 5.] usually display when they come in contact with the smaller portions of the Almighty's universe. He was very condescending and "granted us a short interview." He is president of the New Orleans & Jackson Railroad and has his office in a fine marble-front building in the wealthiest part of the city. He made little or no reference to the war but confined his conversation to the commercial convention and the condition of the railroads. From what he said and our own experience [as a passenger] we concluded that nearly all the railroads in the South were almost as bad stock to invest in as Southern Confederacy bonds. Nearly every one had borrowed money in the North before the war, and when the Confederacy confiscated all moneys due Northern creditors they paid these sums to "the powers that were"; and being now obliged to pay these debts to the lawful creditors, they have become poor as a church mouse. Beauregard was made president of the railroad because people along the [interstate] line were rebels, and the road would be more popular with a rebel general at its head. As we did not deem it such a "tremendous honor" to wait upon the man who had caused so much needless bloodshed and as he seemed to think we were favored with the smiles of a great and noble man while we remained in his office, we thought best to bid him goodbye. He invited us to call again, which we may possibly do if by that means we can get a free pass over the New Orleans & Jackson Railroad.

From General Beauregard's office we went to the outskirts of the city to see how fared the canals and drains which General Butler ordered dug [in 1862] when he kept the pestilential yellow fever out of the city. We found them partially filled with filthy mud, while the top of the black water was covered with a thick scum of yellow-blue color. The stench from them was nearly suffocating, and we made haste to get on the windward side to avoid a retreat toward the city. The city is on a marsh that is much lower than the river, and stagnant water would stand here at any time of the year, making it sickly if there were not other aggravating causes. But when the offal and filth of the

city is carelessly thrown into these fever-breed-
ing sloughs and left to decompose, the effect is
terrible. One of the most rabid rebels we have met
in the South went with us to visit the suburbs, and
although he said all the bad things and told all
the lies he could get into the hour we were with
him about General Butler [Among Butler's adminis-
trative acts was his "General Order No. 28" issued
in the late spring of 1862, which stated: "When any
female shall, by word or gesture, or movement, insult or show contempt for any officer or soldier
of the United States, she shall be regarded and
held liable to be treated as a woman of the town
plying her avocation." The order brewed an inter-
national storm of indignation and it was removed
in December of that year.] yet when we asked why
the city was not kept as neat and these drains as
clean as they were during the [unpopular] military
rule of General Butler [May to December, 1862], he
expressed his idea of the incompetency of the city
government in very strong terms.

"I heartily wish he was back here," said he, "to
pull these city officials over the coals. Why, the
only healthy year this city ever saw was when he
was here to make these lazy fellows toe the mark.
As much as I hate him I wish he was back, and would
vote for him in a minute."

"I hardly think he would run well for mayor,"
said we, jokingly.

"Yes, he would though," said he. "The people
would all vote for him just to spite the present
incompetents."

Later in the day after we had returned to the St.
Charles Hotel we had some conversation with another hater of Butler, and when we referred to the
recent action of the Legislature in licensing gambling houses, lottery schemes [General Beauregard
was supervisor of drawings], and such places, he
exclaimed:

"Well, after all is said, Butler did one good
thing for the city in suppressing crime. You may
not believe it, sir, but he renovated this city,
and a rowdy dared not stay here. Really I wish he
could be in command here long enough to clean out
these gambling dens."

So it was everywhere we went. Men cursed Butler,

wished him all manner of evil, wanted to fight us for refusing to "see it in that light"; yet, each admitted that he wished the General was back to summarily cure some evil they hated.

One day, as we were wandering around the suburbs of the city, looking for magnolia and orange blossoms, we found a stout Negro about thirty years old, digging away in a very large field. He asked us the time of day, and we turned to talk with him. He seemed very intelligent, and told us that he could read and write. After learning that forty acres of this very valuable land belonged to him, we inquired how he came to buy it.

"I tell yer," said he, "it was mighty hard work at first; but I got a little and saved a little. I bought two acres, and the next year paid for three more, and so on until I got forty acres. Land was awful cheap then. But now I couldn't earn enough on my whole forty acres to buy another acre; it has gone up so."

"Does any of this land alongside here belong to colored men?"

"Oh, yes! Lots and lots of it. You see long ago General Butler was down South, and he told us colored folks this way—says he, 'The colored folks are going to be free. They must be free. Now if they will learn to read and write, they will be practically men and women like white folks.' Then he said, 'If now you will go to work and earn, no matter how little, and lay it by until you get a little more, and then buy land, as you will some day, then you will be free like white folks.' He said a darkey with no money was mighty poor, but if he had money and land he would be as good as other folks. So, you see, some of us with nothing but our hands to do with first said we would try it. And after trucking [growing vegetables for market] and working at the cane and potatoes we got a little, and when we see the chance we got a white man to buy for us; and now here we are. One man over there on the shell road is worth fully thirty thousand dollars. His land has gone up so."

We wished him much success, and went on with our search, thinking what a condition the country would have been in had there been no General Butler. Cross out his work and what would the war have been? [In 1869 Butler was in Washington as a representative from Massachusetts.]

At one of the hotels in New Orleans we met a company of Northern health-seekers, and among them was a member of the 52nd Massachusetts who was traveling for his health. He was well acquainted with the city [He had been on duty there during the war.], and we went out to the old camp grounds together. But cotton and sugar then covered the spots, and it was with difficulty that we found them. With him we visited the ruins of Forts Jackson and St. Phillip [downriver near the delta. During the war they were important forts in the defense of New Orleans, although situated facing each other ninety miles below the city. See Lew Dietz, "Deep Delta Journey," *Ford Times* (February 1967), p. 2-6, and J. Cutler Andrews, *The North Reports the Civil War* (Pittsburgh: U. of Pittsburgh Press, 1955), pp. 236-242.]

BATON ROUGE

Our stay in Baton Rouge was very short and on the whole rather dissatisfactory, on account of the driving rain. We visited, however, the still entire walls of the beautiful [Gothic-style] State House [Old State Capitol] and regretted the sacrilegious act which left them so black, dreary, and bare. [It was burned during the war.] We went out to the Magnolia Cemetery and from thence to the National Cemetery, and the Catholic burying ground to view the field so well remembered, no doubt, by the 30th Massachusetts [Infantry] where the brave little garrison [of about twenty-five hundred men] under [Brigadier General Thomas] Williams defended the city [in August, 1862] against a superior rebel force under [Brigadier] General Daniel Ruggles [formerly] of Massachusetts, and General Charles Clark of Mississippi. The buildings bore the scars of conflict and the trees had not outgrown their wounds; but otherwise everything appeared fresh, thrifty, and blooming. The town bears sad marks of its captivity, and it will take years to recuperate. It may, and doubtless will, exceed its former business condition in a short time. But its beauty—the pride of the South—its flowers, trees, vines, and fruit will not come again soon. A garrison of [Federal] soldiers is still kept in the barracks near the town, although for what purpose it would puzzle a Boston lawyer to tell.

The Legislature, owing to the destruction of the State House, meets in New Orleans—thus depriving the city of much of that prestige which it had before the war. [When the capitol was rebuilt in 1882 the State offices were returned to Baton Rouge.] Many of the rich men are selling out and moving to New Orleans. And as each is usually bought out by several men there is an increase in population without a corresponding increase in wealth. Yankees are coming in, and the ways of trade are fast being revolutionized. Negroes own fine houses and large plantations, much to the surprise of their old masters, and the work of the new era has begun.

PORT HUDSON

[Correspondent Conwell traveled by steamer up the Mississippi from New Orleans and Baton Rouge to his next stop, Port Hudson, La. From the boat landing he walked with his baggage to a shanty-like hotel.]

At Port Hudson there were about a dozen buildings, two of which were grocery stores. Between and around these one-story slab houses ran the ditches and lines of earthworks thrown up during the war. Some little patches of ground between the houses were under cultivation, but the soil appeared too barren and sandy to make a fit return for the labor spent upon it. In several of the ruined ditches, which had not been filled since the war, we saw squads of ragged dirty children making mud pies and throwing stones at the ducks. We marked the contrast between this innocent scene and that when [Union General Nathaniel P.] Banks and his men lay out in the edge of the woods yonder [during their six-weeks' siege of Port Hudson in the summer of 1863]. Several men were sitting on the grocery steps talking about the crops, and we ventured to inquire the direction to the National Cemetery [of Port Hudson].

"We don't know nothin' about yer National Cemeteries," said a long, lank, dirty Southerner, scowling, and making an impatient gesture with his hand. [Only Union soldiers are buried in National Cemeteries.]

"I supposed it was near this place," said we, eyeing another member of the party, who appeared a little better natured;but before he could answer, the tall specimen of Southern chivalry arose to his feet in a fury and demanded of us why we dared to intrude upon a private party, and if we did not know it was dangerous to tread on a Southern man's heels. "I do not think I insult any person by inquiring for the grave of a friend," said we, fast losing our temper.

"You are a —— Yankee,and that is the worst thing I can say about you, and your room is better than your company," said another man, taking the first speaker's part.

"Is there not in this company a man who is gentleman enough to tell me where the soldiers' cemetery is?" again asked we, fully determined to stay until we had received a civil answer. No one replied.

Feeling that this was a free country and that we had as much right to the grocery steps as they, we sat down beside them, resolved to imitate the example of General Banks who,when he found a direct assault to be useless,proceeded deliberately to a regular siege. While we took up a piece of barrel hoop and began to whittle, Yankee fashion, they tried to go on with their conversation about the crops, the flood, old Ogleby's mare, and the last fox hunt. But they were evidently uneasy,and their remarks were unconnected and, at times, unintelligible to themselves. At last the conversation ceased altogether. Some looked at the ground;others eyed us sharply while our long-haired enemy was trying to whistle "Dixie"; and we endeavored to keep time with our jack knife.

At last, all out of patience, the company arose to their feet and gathered around in front of us, while one demanded if we wanted to "get into a d—d big fight!"

We merely remarked that we had asked all the questions we should and that we were now willing that they should ask some themselves and kept on whittling.

"See here, stranger, I'll bust yer head if yer don't leave!" shouted a short man, pushing the others aside and squaring off before us. We whittled on.

"Ain't yer going to leave?" shouted he,bringing his arms akimbo. We whittled as before.

"You are a coward, a thief, a liar, a Yankee!" yelled he, leaning over to spit the words at us like a copperhead (snake). We whittled faster.

"You darsent fight!" shouted a half dozen who loved to see a fight but acted as though they should not like to be in one themselves.

"Ain't yer going to fight?" said our pugilistic enemy. We only whittled.

"Come, fellers, let's don't fuss any more with him. He's a fool. Let's let him go. He's a harmless Yankee anyhow," said one starting across the street toward the other grocery.

One after another they dispersed, leaving us to finish the piece of hoop alone. Soon afterward the storekeeper came out in a very obliging way,showed us where the cemetery was situated, and hoped we wouldn't mind those red-hot rebels, as the country was cursed by them, and it was not safe for a man to let his Union sentiments be known. The whole company rushed out of the other grocery, as we clambered over the ruins of an old fort on our way to the cemetery and[those rebels]rather impolitely wished every Yankee "was buried in the d—d old graveyard out in the woods."

The National Cemetery is situated near the edge of the woods, about a mile from the river, and on the very spot where fell so many brave soldiers [in an unsuccessful assault]on the 14th of June,1863. But its condition does not reflect much credit upon the United States government and gives cause for sneers and ridicule to those rebels living near, and they do not fail to take advantage of it. There are no walks, no flowers, and but an excuse for a flag. Many of the head-boards have no inscriptions on them, while many graves of known men have not even a head-board to mark the spot. [A total of 3,827 men are interred, 3,239 unknown.] Nothing can stir our blood so soon to a fever heat as the neglect of the government to protect and care for the graves of its defenders. Especially where they lie in a strange land surrounded by a people that hate them and the principles for which they fought.

We like, whenever we enter a cemetery filled with brave soldiers, to repeat those thrilling words [of the Kentucky poet Theodore O'Hara in his "Bivouac of the Dead":]

On Fame's eternal camping-ground
Their silent tents are spread,
And Glory guards, with solemn round,
The bivouac of the dead.

The fields about the cemetery are cultivated in a way that surprises the stranger, and the first question we asked of the crippled old darkey at the cemetery was in regard to the ownership of the land. The land for a half mile around was covered with fallen timber during the war, which was cut down by the rebels to make an *abattis* for their breastworks. But it is now cleared and ploughed under the hand of freed black labor, and crops of cotton and King Corn [successor to King Cotton] now sway on the plain like the waves of a lake. The heavy breastworks behind which the rebels stood when they were, able to repulse the brave attacks of our troops are still standing and serve to divide the plantation into sections of about the right size to let to individuals on shares. They are, however, gradually sliding down before the hoe and plough, and in five or six years at most will be entirely obliterated.

This whole plantation of nearly two thousand acres is owned by a Mr. Smith of Ohio and is cultivated by Negroes under the charge of his son and Mr. William R. Bates. When these gentlemen first came to the place, they were threatened with all manner of evil by the rebellious population of the little town above them. But they went their way, asking nothing, taking nothing, and are now doubtless making more money than all the rest of the town together. Several times the other farmers wished to make a combination with Mr. Bates which should exclude Negro labor entirely from the place. But as the Negroes had fled to him for protection and had settled on his farm in such numbers, Mr. Bates let land to them on shares, getting an immense profit from his land, while the acres all about him grew up to weeds and brush for the need of laborers to cultivate it. The Negroes, too, are

making money and seem more contented and happy than
at any other place we have seen in the South. This
one family, with its Northern ways and habits, its
modern improvements, and its noble sister that is
teaching the Negroes, will soon produce a wonderful change in the appearance of both people and
land. The influence of the Yankees' progressive
ideas will soon reconstruct the South, in spite of
the prejudices and dislikes that are now seen and
felt.

From the cemetery we went down into the belt of
woods, thinking that it might be interesting to the
New England boys to read how their old camping
grounds now look. [One of them, Charles H. Taylor,
in 1869 private secretary (with honorary rank of
colonel) to Governor William Claflin of Massachusetts, had served as a private soldier and been
wounded at Port Hudson in 1863. He had been a
printer and reporter on the *Traveller*, hence a jour-
nalistic colleague of young Conwell.] Peaches they
must have had in abundance [in 1863]. For every
camp ground, and especially those of the 8th and
16th New Hampshire, the 4th, 30th, 31st, and 53d
Massachusetts [Infantry] is now covered with a dense
thicket of peach trees that have grown from the
peach stones thrown away during the [summer] siege.
The other camp grounds, except those of the 2d, 4th,
and 13th Massachusetts Batteries [Light Artillery],
we could not find, so changed has the face of nature become. Thousands of bushels of peaches will
ripen this year where six years ago was a field of
white tents and the scene of guard mounting and
dress parade. The change in the camp grounds is
no greater than the change everywhere about Port
Hudson: no tents, no guns, no flags, no artillery,
infantry, or cavalry; no wagon trains or ambulances;
no gunboats, no war. All covered with crops; the
[Mississippi] river sweeps on "unvexed to the sea"
[Abraham Lincoln, August 26, 1863, in letter to
Honorable James C. Conkling, of Springfield, Illinois.]; the sun bleaches the plains; and a sweet,
lasting peace has come.

The Confederate dead at Port Hudson were left
where they fell, and the ploughshare of the cotton
planter turns up many a skeleton that was buried
after the siege. The active waters of the old Mis-

sissippi as they whirl and foam in the eddy in front of the lower fort have worn away the banks and gradually exposed coffins that after a while slide into the bubbling foam to travel into the dark, mysterious unknown. The day we were there the black bones that once were soldiers' feet stuck out of the caving bank, becoming more and more exposed each hour, following the hundreds that had been drawn from their graves near them at the silent demand of the river. Poor mortals! As unsettled in death as in life! No rest! not even for their bones!

We were told here that all of the old planters of Louisiana have kept a careful account of the number and value of their slaves in order that their bills may be ready when the government comes to pay for their slaves, as they think it will some day. Some are foolish enough to suppose that an arrangement might somehow be made with England, by which the English would get this as an offset for the [still unsettled] Alabama Claims [damages claimed by the United States against England for shipping losses caused by British-made cruisers used by the Confederacy], and the slaveholders get the pay for their human property which the government took from them. We have since seen a bill all regularly made out, i.e., according to the planter's notion, which the signer hoped to get honored some day at the national treasury. As but few of our readers have seen such a document we will give it in full:

The Federal Authorities,
To Nathan Foeling, Dr.

For the following named slaves, unlawfully taken away from the undersigned, and given their liberty, against the right of their owner and contrary to the consistent judgement of all Christian men and women:

Joseph, 55 years old, with one eye, and a little lame, was offered $500 for him in 1860, but charge the authorities for him only $230

Caleb, about 32 years old, consumptive some, but not bad...................... $600

Sam, a boy about 23, very lively, was
kicked by a horse in the back, but it
does not affect his value as a field hand.. $900

Sarah, aged 40, house servant, neat
and quick............................... $500

Jim, a stout fellow, weighs 190 pounds,
aged 29, good disposition, will work
without an overseer.................... $2200

Dinah, a girl 10 years old, very
lively and affectionate............... $400

Old Solomon, aged 70, good for pulling
corn and handy about a cotton gin....... $300

Betsey, wife of Caleb, aged 30, has
sound teeth and lively fingers, is
healthy................................ $800

Betsey and John, her children, aged 3
and 5, all plump, $100 each............ $200

Verna, a stout house-girl, very neat
and modest, mostly white, and of sweet
disposition; a first-class hand for a
gentleman's family as housemaid........ $1800

The above is a true bill, at a figure much below
the actual value, of my slaves taken by the Federal
authorities, for which I demand payment.

Nathan Foeling

The idea that one gets of Port Hudson by the
stories which have been told about it and the his-
tories which have been written of its siege and
capture is at once put to flight by a visit to the
unromantic spot. As we were about to take the
steamer [to go up the river toward Natchez and
Vicksburg] we inquired of a gentleman what the inhabitants did to pass away time.

"Suck our thumbs," said he, promptly.

"Don't you have any parties, balls, excursions,
or pleasure meetings?" said we.

"Oh, yes, now and then," he replied. "But the
fact is that so many of the young fellows have been
killed off, and husband timber is so mighty scarce,
that it is nigh about the death of a fellow to go

to a party. There never fails to be three girls
to one fellow,and such a squirming, kissing, hugging as we do get! Oh! I've sworn off,and hereafter shall not trust myself within a mile of a
kissing party."
"Poor things!"thought we, as we stepped on board
the steamer, leaving Port Hudson, with its slab
hotel,one-horse,wooden-track railroad [which runs
to Clinton],its dilapidated rifle pits, and blustering secessionists, to the mercy of the scorching sun.

ARISTOCRATIC HOSPITALITY

[Twenty-six-year-old Conwell's roguish description of his weekend at an elegant Mississippi residence locates it in or close to Port Gibson, below Vicksburg. There the lonesome, tired, hungry,
and feature-eager Boston reporter—between Saturday, May 8 and Monday, May 10—was entertained by
a family who resided in that community famous for
its lovely prewar mansions including "Gage House,"
"Windsor," and "Serenity." The picturesque old
town (spared by invading Union General Grant in
1863 with the words,"It's too beautiful to burn,")
had a twelve-mile shuttle line, the Port Gibson
Railroad,linking it with Grand Gulf on the Mississippi near its confluence with the Big Black. Only
a few miles upstream from the two terminal towns
was the Jefferson Davis plantation, on the south
side of Hurricane Island, which Conwell said he
visited by boat the next day, Tuesday, before he
reached Vicksburg.]
Not many days ago, and at a place not a thousand
miles from Vicksburg, a fierce-looking moustache,
with a man attached to it,invited us to dine with
it. So urgent was his invitation and so much of
an honor would he deem our company that we consented to go. We did not wish to accept his invitation and had much rather eat our corn bread
and bacon at the hotel than partake of nature's
richest viands in the house of a stranger. Yet
there was no such thing as refusing, and so we
went.
The moustache stood in the doorway of a splendid
[ante-bellum] mansion as we approached, and con-
descendingly sent his "nigger" to open the gate
and show us up the labyrinth-like pathway which

led around the flower beds to the porch.

"I am exceedingly happy to see you, Sir!" exclaimed our host, extending both his hands and almost pulling us up into the porch.

"This is my daughter D——and this is my daughter M——," said he,motioning toward some fine jewelry, paint, and feathers, supported by two forms that looked for all the world like wasps standing on their tails, but which, in the South, are often called "young ladies." The mustache gave a dignified grin; the feathers bobbed, creases came in the paint, and we walked into the parlor of the chivalrous Southron feeling like an alligator we saw [downstream] at Baton Rouge trying to climb a tree. However, we soon felt our awkwardness clearing away before the "make-yourself-at-home" demeanor of our host. After the compliments of the day were passed, and we had been introduced to a thin, delicate lady with a small voice [the wife of the moustache?], a song was proposed, and the paint and jewelry seated itself sideways at the piano [and asked:]

"Shall I play 'Dixie,' Pa?"

"No! No!" quickly responded our host, "give us a National air."

"I'm sure,Pa,you must know I can't play National airs; no one plays them here."

"Well, give us 'Willie's on the blue, black—or dark—sea.'" [Stephen Foster's "Willie my Brave" was then popular,as were several other mournful"Willie" songs. But the one Conwell's host requested must have been "Willie's on the Dark Blue Sea," written and composed by H. S. Thompson and published in 1853 by Oliver Ditson of Boston.It has five stanzas and two choruses and was issued by various publishers and printers in both sheet-music and song-sheet formats.]

"That is the next thing to the 'Star Spangled Banner.' Isn't it, Mr. Correspondent?"

"We would be happy to hear anything," said we, looking over the [sheet] music and selecting from the small pile [T. M. Sewell's] "Sally Come Up," "Up in a Balloon" [written this year by H. B. Farnie],and [Marshall S.Pike and L.V.H. Crosby's] "De Skeeters Do Bite," wondering if that was the class of music these painted dolls delighted in.

These, and the "Bonnie Blue Flag," "My Maryland," and "Dixie" composed the greater part of the collection. Soon the usual routine of teasing and coaxing was over and the performer began. We were rather pleased with [Will S. Hays's] "Write Me a Letter from Home" and in imitation of the Southern flatterers told the dear performer that it reminded us of [the opera soprano] Madame [Euphrosyne] Parepa-Rosa [then touring the United States]. But we did not say "by contrast."

After the singing, the conversation turned upon the state of the South. Our host became considerably excited as the discussion went on and at last rose to his feet, exclaiming:

"That's the way it always has been. The South is slandered by the North. You say you have been everywhere treated kindly; and that is, as I know, the testimony of every Northern man that comes here. We have done rebelling. We say, 'It's all right now.' Come among us; we will receive you kindly and do all we can for you. Here's my daughters; as good girls as ever lived, and not bad looking, either. Now the time has been when we wouldn't have a Yankee on this estate. But now—now—the young sprigs are killed off—and—and—we feel like inviting others to take their places. We are human. We like society, and we love our Northern brethren. We receive them as we do you, sir, with open arms. The people of the great and noble North are our friends, and we have nothing but the purest love for them."

Here he was interrupted by the tea bell, and we went to the feast of "good things" determined that if we could not feel quite at home in that society, we would at least enjoy one square meal. How we got through the evening and the night—for we could not break away—we cannot tell. Vague memories of songs, piano, guitar, little stories, the recital of Mother Goose, a cup of coffee, and a soft bed is all we distinctly recall. But when breakfast was over, which we swallowed in company with our host only, and we took a leave, which was exceedingly affectionate on his part, we drew a long sigh of relief and rehearsed mentally a eulogy on the spirit of freedom. We distinctly remember feeling, as we passed out of the iron gate which the same colored individual closed, a strong temptation to turn and inscribe on the panel those classic words, "Who enters here leaves all hope behind" [A variation of Dante's "Inferno": "Leave all hope,ye that enter."].

During our stay in that place [in and around Port Gibson] we met our host often, and he was always very pleasant and agreeable. We learned also that he was trying hard to get the office of Internal Revenue Collector. The morning when we intended to take our departure, our friend came down to see us off and wished us a happy journey and a long life as the train [for Grand Gulf] started. Owing to an accident, the train did not get far from the depot and in company with other passengers we walked back to the [Port Gibson] station. On going into the passenger room to deposit our baggage, we saw our friend with his back toward us engaged in loud and earnest conversation with a neighbor. Imagine our chagrin when as we came nearer to them, we heard the following conversation almost verbatim:

"As for me," said the neighbor, "I love the South too much to fraternize with her enemies."

"Nor I, nor I!" exclaimed our host, "unless I see that I can make something out of him. The nigger brings a pail of swill, you know, when we wish to catch the pig and get his bacon."

"But what in the —— could you want of that radical from Boston?" inquired the neighbor.

"I want him to say a good word for me in the radical papers. That's just what I want. I may need them to use in Washington. As for the d—d fool of a Yankee himself, to tell the truth, I felt like cutting his throat every time I looked at him. I would just like to hang up every cussed Yankee that comes down here. For they only stir up the niggers to insolence and deviltry."

"Well, maybe you can stomach them, but I can't; and I reckon it will be some time before I'll introduce one, right from Boston, to my young ladies," said the neighbor, sarcastically.

Upon this we turned hastily away, with our minds made up that no moustache, no jewelry, no paint, no waterfalls, no feathers, no sleepy eyes, nor anything would ever get us into another aristocratic mansion where the "pure love of the North" is dealt out for newspaper puffs.

VICKSBURG

The Roman, who could boast of seven hills and the throne they sustained, was no more vainglorious than were the aristocratic citizens of Vicksburg ["The Gibraltar of the Confederacy"] in 1860. They were not many in numbers, but they felt as though Vicksburg might at some future day "rule the world." Each family had two servants to each member in the mansion and hundreds at work in the fields. They could live like princes and do nothing. They lay in bed late in the morning, sat in the shade till evening, were driven out [in carriages] by their servants at night, and returning, danced till midnight. The ladies were too proud to stoop for a handkerchief and had servants to pick it up and to carry the trails of their dresses. The men, for want of better occupation, walloped niggers, fawned on the ladies, and fought duels.

But the location of the city was hardly pleasant or convenient. Let a farmer place twenty or thirty haystacks on the banks of a river as close together as they can stand, and he will have a facsimile of the hills upon and among which stood Vicksburg. The streets cut through between these hills were very narrow and at places were hemmed in by perpendicular banks of sand forty feet high. At other places, where the ravines crossed, deep caverns yawned upon the dizzy traveller as he dared to look down the embankment. The dwellings and stores were set into the sides of hills or on their tops, while in many cases it was sure death to fall or leap from the porch into the street below. A few brick buildings along the river bank contained the greater part of the merchandise, except perhaps in the open spaces where the cotton was piled for shipment to New Orleans.

At that time Cotton was King. A Southerner could whip three Yankees. The "nigger" had no rights which the white man was bound to respect. Jeff Davis often drove up—or, rather, his darkey drove—from his plantation down the [Mississippi] river and made bargains with the boats to land at his

place to take off cotton. He often took drinks
with his older brother, Joe [Joseph Emory]. Jeff
talked politics then and tried to induce his brother
to go into the Confederacy business. It might do
for Jeff but not for Joe. So his brother kept out.
Three years. Vicksburg in war [in 1863]. A
grand sight it must have been! The tops of the
numerous hills [or cliffs] covered with breastworks and these surmounted with long dark rows of
cannon; the Confederate flag, ragged and dirty,
flying from the isolated courthouse; the long line
of gunboats down the river lying listlessly at
anchor [An ironclad gunboat, the *Cairo* of the Union
navy, was discovered recently in the Yazoo River
near Vicksburg. When completely restored, it will
be exhibited in a naval museum in that city.]; the
mortar fleet in the river across the peninsula;
the yellow line of earth being thrown from the
canal [being dug] by the United States soldiers;
the wide dark [Mississippi] river moving slowly
on to the Gulf; the silent city among the hills;
the deserted levee and unoccupied warehouses then
under fire; when the smoke of the echoing guns
almost hid the gunboats and mortar fleet; when
shrieking shells descended upon the dwellings, the
warehouses, the streets, the hills, the forts, everywhere; when the smoke of burning buildings curled
up to the bright skies and left a shadow over the
city; when each hilltop belched flame and smoke
and iron; when the city shook until the sandy hills
began to crumble upon the streets and houses in huge
avalanches; when all the inhabitants [several thou-
sands] were crowded into caves dug in the perpendicular [loess] banks; when the thick cloud of smoke
encircling the city in the distance showed where
[General] Grant's lines were engaged; and when the
dead were too thick in the streets to bury and the
wounded too many to care for; when death, suffering,
sorrow, terror were the sacrifices demanded of the
people who had transgressed the commands of a just
God.

How they must have suffered! Living in holes
which caved in upon them, burying them alive; living
on rats, mules, and dogs; constantly in terror of
mortar shells, which fell about the mouths of their
caves and often rolled in to burst, kill, and mangle;

when legless men, bleeding and uncared for, lay
upon the hillsides,armless women shrieked in pain
for help from the caverns; when the descent of an
avalanche mercifully took from the inhabitants a
few mouths that they would otherwise have been
obliged to feed; when horrid snakes and lizards
crawled over the sleepers at night; when, at last,
starved and ragged, made insane by weeks of terror
and suspense, [Lieutenant]General [John C.]Pember-
ton, who had made a "brave defense," when all but he
was starving, surrendered them [on July 4, 1863]
into the hands of [Union General]Grant,the "fiendish Yankee."

Vicksburg today [in 1869]is a quiet little town
of some little commercial importance and is made
lively by the frequent arrivals of steamboats from
St. Louis [to the north] or New Orleans [to the
south]. The buildings show the marks of the great
siege and in many places patch-work covers the
greater part of the structures. The hundreds of
caves in the sides of the hills are still open and
bring to mind the accounts of suffering there.
Many, however, have caved in, and in some places
the whole side of the hill came down into the street
at the same time.

One of these caves, opened a few weeks ago,* was
found to contain the bones of a whole family who
had been suffocated there during the siege. The
cannons have all been removed, but the rifle pits
and earth forts still remain on the hill tops.
The spot where Grant and Pemberton consulted upon
the terms of surrender, which was then surrounded
by trees and shaded by the branches of a large oak,
is now in an open field,cultivated by a Negro who
fought there. The marble monument, raised to mark
the spot, was so hacked by relic-seekers that it
had been removed, and a ten-inch Columbiad gun
reared in its place, upon which is engraved the
words:

The Site Where Gen. U. S. Grant
Arranged the Terms of Surrender with
Lt. Gen. Pemberton

The graves of the Northern soldiers, which were
thickly strewn over the hillsides and along the

ravines, have been opened and the bodies taken to the [National] Cemetery [established in 1865] just above the city on the bank of the [Mississippi] river. [Of the 16,615 now buried there, 12,716 are unknown soldiers.] The Confederate graves are ploughed over and obliterated.

The canal [Grant's Canal across the De Soto Peninsula], which took so much time and labor to excavate, is now filled with sand and flood wood deposited by the overflowing Mississippi.

The Southern chivalry, either refusing "to hire a nigger" or unable to get them, are now obliged to carry their own trails [garment trains], drive their own or borrowed horses, and turn to the right when they meet a colored citizen of African descent. Yankees are working into the trade and building some new stores while the Negroes are industrious and happy, having homes and schools of their own. A combination of the landowners, who will not sell a foot of land to a Negro, at present hinders the full exercise of their enterprising spirit; but this cannot last long. The junk shops are full of old pieces of shell and tons of bullets, which will soon be shipped away and recast into stoves, roofing, or perhaps into "ploughshares and pruning-hooks" [Isaiah II:4.] The glorious old flag floats proudly from the staff over the National dead and from the top of the barracks in the city, where the garrison of soldiers now remain.

The silent, smooth old Mississippi moves majestically on, carrying up and down the commerce of a mighty nation. No batteries frown from its banks; no rebel flags fly from the bluffs; all speaks of peace. That peace which "flows like a river" [Isaiah 48:18 and 66:12.] must soon come, and the nation become the "home of the free" [Variation of Francis Scott Key's "The Star Spangled Banner."] which the soldiers of the nation fought to make it. The Fourth of July was a fitting date for rebels against the government founded on that day to surrender, and may the nation founded in '76 and preserved in '63 see many hundred years before another hand is raised against it.

[On Decoration Day] don't forget the dead that died and were buried away from home. [See Florence

Ogden's article,"The Blue and the Gray: The Story
of Decoration Day" in *DAR Magazine* (May 1968), p.
548 ff.] Dedicate the wreath to them which you
hang upon the monument. We have endeavored to make
arrangements with the cemetery keepers to have the
graves of the Massachusetts and New Hampshire dead
decorated with flowers on that day. [The *Traveller*
circulates in both states.] We would like to have
made it universal that no patriot's grave might go
without a tribute. But, alas! Many will lie in
their cold graves unnoticed, but we hope they or
their deeds are not forgotten. For ourself,we will
decorate the graves of our comrades on that day and
strew flowers over as many as we possibly can,and
we ask of the patriotic assemblies who meet on that
day that they remember in some befitting manner
the dead who sleep "in a strange land"[Exodus 2:22].
One hundred and fifty thousand Northern dead lie
in the South, and nearly two-thirds of them [are]
"Unknown"; you must not forget them.
   "He mourns the dead who lives as they desire."
[Edward Young, "Night Thoughts."]
   We cannot close this letter without [further]
reference to Jeff Davis's plantation["Briarfield"]
which we visited yesterday [May 11]. It lies on
the banks of the Mississippi, about thirty miles
below Vicksburg [on Hurricane Island] and is an
exceedingly lovely place. Jeff never owned it
himself, though he staid upon it from 1832 until
1861. It belonged to his brother, Joe, who lives
[He died in 1870.] in Vicksburg and gave Jeff the
use of it (or what is more likely, Joe managed to
cook up a title [to the land] when he was pardoned
and he saw that Jeff's property was to be confiscated by the government). The buildings all remain
as they were when Jeff left, except a few Negro
quarters that have been torn down. An old Negro
that used to be one of Jeff's slaves now leases
the plantation of Joe for ten thousand dollars a
year and hires a hundred and fifty hands to work
it. Not a white man is to be seen about the place.
Strange as it may seem to Mr. Davis,his old slave
is making money fast and feels as proud as any
white man "libin in ole Jeff's parlor dese days."
The whole plantation of several thousand acres is
planted to cotton, which appears very promising,

and, from this plantation, cotton enough will be produced to run a mill in Lowell [Massachusetts] for weeks.

"We jist lets old Massa Jeff make political speeches an' we'll see dat de cotton grows," said the darkey who showed us about. "Golly, who'd sposed dat dis chile would ben free and libin on dis yer plantation wid my Dolly dar? yah! yah! yah! ole Jeff's cum to grief shuah. He'd be hoppin' mad, dough, to see dis yer nigger here. Yah! yah! yah!"

We left him laughing on the shore and moved off to the boat, moralizing upon the mutability of human events.

TWO STEAMER FIGHTS

Three days ago a Boston man [Conwell] was on board the steamboat *Indiana* [a 1527-ton sidewheeler], which runs between New Orleans and Cincinnati, and, having nothing else to do, employed himself in watching the movements of the crew. One of the colored boatmen was very slow and sluggish and often called down upon him a shower of red-hot curses from the mate. Finally the mate got so angry that he told the man to leave and offered him his pay for the half month, $4. The colored man said he would do the best he could, but he wished to work on under his contract. The mate flew in a fury at the refusal to take his pay, which would be virtually annuling the contract, and with his lighted lantern struck the Negro over the head, cutting his face terribly and covering him with [kerosene] oil. The Boston man, like everybody else, looked on in silence. But he could not avoid making the determination never to witness again such brutality without interfering.

At Helena, Arkansas, the Boston man stopped and took another boat for Fort Pillow [on the western edge of Tennessee]. On this boat was a mulatto man who had been an orderly sergeant in the Federal Army and was quite intelligent and gave the Boston man a great deal of information. The mate of the boat abused all the men and was constantly pulling them about and cursing them in a most disgusting manner.

At last, for some neglect of duty or failure to comprehend his commands, the mate got exceedingly angry with the mulatto,and, seizing a window sash filled with glass an eighth of an inch thick, he raised it to strike the mulatto. The latter dodged the blow and ran up the gangway and,backing into a corner near the Boston man,entreated the mate not to strike him "wid dat glass." The mate rushed at him like a demon and with one stroke smashed the sash and glass over the offending man's head,cutting huge gashes in his cheeks and forehead and rendering him for a moment senseless. The mate again lifted the remnant of the sash over his head for another blow,when the Boston man caught the sash from behind saying at the same time coolly:

"Don't you strike that man again."

"Who in the devil are you?" almost screamed the angry man.

"No matter, don't you strike that man again."

"By——I'll shoot h—l out of you——," said the mate, pulling out his revolver and shaking it in the face of the Boston man.

"You know, sir, that you dare not shoot me," said the latter coolly, "so put up your revolver."

By this time a crowd had gathered around and "shoot him!" "shoot him!" echoed on every side. The Boston man learned afterward that there was not another [Northern] man on the boat.

"Shoot him by—— or I will!" exclaimed a little short man on one side of the crowd.

"Let's all have a hack at him," said another, and in an instant no less than twelve pistols or revolvers were displayed.

"He's a cussed Yankee. I know his phiz. He's down here preachin' insurrection among the niggers. Shoot him, mate, or we will."

"So ho! so ho!" sneered the Yankee, "things have changed since the war, somewhat, I guess. Now, gentlemen, I see it takes twelve Southerners to shoot one unarmed Yankee."

This set them on fire,and one burly fellow cocked his revolver, saying, "If the mate was a d—d coward I'm not afraid to shoot any Yankee in the country."

Just then a lady, who was evidently of Northern birth, came up to the crowd and, putting out both

of her index fingers toward them, made an awful
scowl and exclaimed: "S-h-a-m-e, s-h-a-m-e on you.
Twelve stout men attack an unarmed man with revolvers! Shame! shame!"

All of the party, including the mate, began to
look sheepish, and as the captain came rushing up
to the spot they slunk away. The mate, however,
muttered something about "seeing this man" again.
The lady had disappeared in the meantime, otherwise your Boston man might have neen induced to
marry her on the spot. When the excitement had
somewhat abated, the captain asked the Boston man
what was the matter. It was explained to him,
together with the information that a complaint
would be lodged against the assailants at the next
landing. This information was communicated doubtless to them, for, after supper one came up to
the Boston man and offered his hand, saying:

"Stranger, we're kind o' ashamed o' that ere
affair a little while ago. Come, come, let's licker,
and call 'em a draw game. What der yer say, ole
feller?"

"I don't drink," said the Yankee.

"Well, take suthin or other and we'll all take
whiskey. Come. Tain't more'n fair yer should
'cept a pollogy."

"It's just here, gentlemen," said the Yankee to
the crowd now gathering around, "I'll accept the
apology. But I want you to understand hereafter
that when you attempt to bully a Yankee that's
carried bullets in his body this five years –
which he received thrashing you fellows out—why,
just recollect that you've got hold of the wrong
chicken."

"Let's licker, let's licker; don't stop to talk,"
interrupted they. The treat passed around, and
"all went merry as a marriage bell" [Lord Byron,
Child Harold's Pilgrimage.].

No, we can't say that. The mulatto, the origin
of this trouble, where was he? Just where the
Negro was at the end of the Civil War, which was
brought on by slavery. Down in the hold among the
rubbish, surrounded by his own sympathizing kind,
bleeding and aching, not daring to say his soul
was his own, fearing to lift his voice or finger
in self-defense, and too ill-informed to appeal to

the laws of that nation to save which he offered his life as a soldier.

FORT PILLOW

It was near sunset when we clambered up the sandy bluff on which Fort Pillow [Tennessee,overlooking the Mississippi] was constructed. The boat gave a shrill whistle and the captain shouted "All right!" and we were left alone on the dreary spot. Far off toward the woods could be seen a few huts whose low roofs and wooden chimneys just appeared above the luxuriant growth of brush and weeds. Nature, as if trying to hide from view the spot where such fiendish deeds were committed, has covered the fields, the [earthwork] fortifications, and even the parade ground with thick foliage.

Up and down, into the ravines and out, lost in the trees and again in the clearing, we wandered about searching for some signs of the battle. Low, overgrown mounds and fallen trees together with a high embankment near the bluff is all that is left of Fort Pillow, the name of which we feel tempted to suppress for the disgrace it entails upon the American people. [His reference is to the so-called "massacre" of April 12, 1864, when the Union-held fort fell in a cavalry assault directed by Confederate General Nathan B. Forrest—who later became Grand Wizard of the Klu Klux Klan.] When the sun was gone and the stars had appeared we twisted our way through the undergrowth and sat down upon the bank to watch the ceaseless motion of the river and pass our time as best we could until the [southbound] steamer for Memphis [Tennessee] should come and take us on board. But as we sat there in the starlight,alone,we could not avoid a glance toward the heavens nor suppress the thought that "God is just but man is unjust" [Henry W. Longfellow, "Evangeline"; line transposed.].

The boat arrived and bore us down the swift current of the deep, mysterious [Mississippi] river; the shores were gloomy and dark; the stars of heaven alone looked cheerful.

MEMPHIS

Of the stirring city of Memphis,so full of trade and treason[it became a Confederate military center in 1861], we can say but little, looking at it as we do from a historical point of view. One serious conflict it saw when[Union Flag Officer Andrew H.] Foote's gunboats attacked the rebel flotilla in front of the town [early in 1862]. But the sunken crafts are all gone,and the men who commanded them were remembered with flowers on the last Confederate Decoration Day.

[At the Planter's Insurance Office in Memphis, Conwell visited General Forrest who was seated "in a large chair,his desk full of papers and his hands full of policies." The *Traveller* correspondent wrote no compliments about the general,adding that "an array of harassing memories and torturing thoughts come with his name."

From Memphis,Conwell evidently rode in the cars of the Memphis & Charleston Railroad(once called the"vertebrae of the Confederacy") eastward to Corinth, Mississippi, which he said he visited. He must have been drawn there by his desire to inspect the present condition of the field at Pittsburg Landing on the Tennessee River, where the Battle of Shiloh (Church)—the first great battle of the war—took place April 6-7, 1862. Whether the subsequent leg of his tour was by rail or by river is unrecorded, but he next appeared at a fort in northern Tennessee.]

FORT DONELSON

Fort Donelson [on the Cumberland River],the spot where General Grant won the first of his laurel crowns[by capturing the fort February 12-16,1862], was a point of especial interest to us,and we took great pains to be left there at such a time that we should have the day before us for exploration. But we were sadly disappointed in the appearance of Fort Donelson—or rather in its non-appearance. [Henry W.] Longfellow's initial line in[his poem] "Evangeline" came unbidden to our lips as we clambered about on the bluffs: "This is the forest primeval." For every trace of war is so effectu-

ally covered by trees that the visitor cannot tell
whether he has found the artificial mounds of wartime or primitive knolls of the forest. There is
a little clearing about the farm house where Grant
established his headquarters,but otherwise all is
overgrown and lost. [The site was made a National
Military Park in 1928.] · Little spots at one side
of the fort, where the fresh earth has recently
been overturned, tell where the brave Illinoisans
"slept their last sleep" [See Lyman Heath's "The
Grave of Bonaparte,"]until transferred to the cemetery. Brave fight was this on both sides! All
day we strolled about Fort Donelson,deriving more
pleasure in thinking on its history than looking
on its disguised location, and at 5 o'clock the
boat came which [took us up the Cumberland River
and] landed us safely in the hilly city of Nashville.

NASHVILLE

One thousand miles north [up from New Orleans to
central Tennessee]from mid-summer to early spring!
One week ago we saw the ripe fruit and the advanced harvest. But today,unopened buds and chilly
winds admonish us that we must live the summer
over again,the summer we enjoyed a few weeks ago.
We have gone back from August to May. From blue-
berries, blackberries, green corn, oranges, and
bananas through a belt of green peas,strawberries,
and lettuce to the flowers of the apple and the
peach. One week ago in the land of sunshine and
peace! Today in the land of storms and Ku-Klux.
[The Klan was organized in 1865 at Pulaski, Tennessee,and centralized in 1867 at Nashville.]
We almost flew up the street to the [State]Cap-
itol, where, with delighted eyes, we viewed again
the scenes of days gone by. The noble structure
[in the style of an Ionic temple], which may well
be the boast of Tennessee and which for beauty of
internal design is excelled only by the capitol at
Washington, stands majestically overlooking the
city, the villages, plains, and rivers as it did
[when we first saw it] in [the summer of] 1864.
Around it lie the ruinous walls, blocks of hewn
marble, and flagstones for the uncompleted pave-

ment; the black ledge crops out here and there along the brow of the hill, just as they were left when the hands at work on the unfinished capitol grounds took occasion to rebel and leave their work for the Confederate Army. [Cf. Trowbridge, John T., "Nashville," *The Desolate South 1865-66*, ed. Gordon Carroll(New York: Duell, Sloan & Pearce, 1956), p. 150.]

But the rifle pits and heavy batteries that our memory associated with the spot and which guarded each pillared entrance to the building are now gone, and the bare ledge looks as innocent as though it never bore upon its back the murderous weapons of death. [In 1862 it was called Fort Johnson, headquarters of Union Army activities.] From the porch where we lingered, to cast our eyes over one of the most beautiful landscapes in America, we turned to the interior and were soon trying our hands at the doubly bolted door of the House of Representatives and the folding gates of the Senate [chamber]. They wouldn't open to us, [and we] left the doors and went upstairs into the galleries. There were the same tapestry-hung walls, the same splendid marble columns, the same curtain chairs, the same rows of marred desks, and the inevitable litter of peanut shucks.

From the Legislative hall we peeped slyly into the Governor's Room. Great change here. New desks on one side—old ones turned about—and everything renovated. From the Governor's Room we went to the Adjutant General's and the Treasurer's offices, and then left the building and hurried down the street to visit the former Deputy Provost Marshall's Office, where so many of the boys used to apply every day for a pass to go to West Nashville or Edgefield. What a change! it was [now, in 1869] a candy shop! And engraved on the fountain were the words, "Tuft's Arctic Soda Fountain, Boston." There were now long striped sticks of candy instead of muskets, confectionary instead of decanters, a Newfoundland dog in place of a pile of champagne bottles, a soda fountain in lieu of a whiskey [bar].

The next building, where the boys who did guard duty used to sit night after night, writing letters, playing games, or relieving their companions on the street corners, is now a lager beer shop, and many there be that go in thereat. [Variation of Holy Bible—Matthew 7:13: "and many there be which go in thereat."].

Nashville does not seem to recover from the effects of the war like many other cities we have seen. Fortifications still stand within a few rods of her streets; old cannons lie about near the river; the forts out on the surrounding hills look fresh and threatening; the depot is filled with cars marked with the old familiar words, "U.S. Military R.R."; boats scarred with shot land at her wharf; the flag of the Union floats over the barracks in West Nashville; the piers of the old [Confederate General Felix K.] Zollicoffer Bridge, destroyed by the rebels, are left in their ruin, while the new suspension bridge spans the river below; the Post Office (Oh, how anxiously have we asked [in 1864?] for letters there!) still occupies its old site, and uniformed regulars and militia still inquire for "news from home."

If the fine [ante-bellum] residences once used as headquarters were guarded now—if sentinels walked the corners—if the old Cumberland Barracks were restored and the Military Academy open as a hospital (in which once lay so many wounded), no other change could counteract the conviction that the iron rule of the military had ceased to exercise its arbitrary powers.

LOOKOUT MOUNTAIN

Oh, the old mountains! How we love to gaze upon them and dream! How our soul fills with unspeakable pleasure as we contemplate the rocky cliffs and the roaring gorges of the mountains! [The cliffs and gorges in the Hampshire Highlands of the Berkshire Hills newspaperman Conwell knew well in his home town, Worthington, Massachusetts.] It is the inspired pleasure which one feels only when he looks upon the mighty works of God. The spirit of the hills and the demons of the mountains! Are they a myth? No. Go! ye unbelievers who laugh at ghost stories and fairy tales; sit beside that sweet waterfall [Now called High Falls, a major attraction of "Rock City" area opened in 1932.] on the cliffy side of Lookout Mountain [1700 feet above Chattanooga and 2,126 feet above sea level] and tell us if ye doubt their existence then. Go! sit on that jutting rock that is bathed with the spray and gaze up at the little stream as it leaps over the rocks forty feet above! and then at the snowy spray-cloud that rolls and floats away, away down among the bushes and trees forty feet below. The stout old trees creak and sway in the winds above, the pines down the mountain side moan, and the waterfall laughs. Away through the trees are those other mountains, shadowy and blue, just veiling the sky of the far-off horizon [across the Tennessee River].

He that can sit here alone, surrounded by these jagged rocks and monumental mountains, and see no German fairies, English ghosts, Arabian [or Persian] peris, or Norwegian demons hath surely no taste for natural beauty nor a fit appreciation of the awe-inspiring works of the Almighty. Deny it, ye who may, the mountains do have souls, and their children, the fairies, do have an influence upon the destinies of men. Else why is it that the men of the mountains are always hardier, happier, and greater lovers of freedom than they of the plains and valleys? Why are the people of the hills more generous, loftier minded, and braver than their brethren of the prairie? If the fairies do not [inspire] their human protégés, how came Switzerland free?

Far, far along the highway of history, who were the conquerors? Who the patrons of civilization? who the martyrs? Men of the mountains! Who march into the city with less education, less capital than their competitors, and so soon lead the march toward the land of plenty and wealth? Who came down from the North and West and on the cragged side of this same mountain gained a Switzerlandish victory? The men of the fairy-filled mountains! Men of the city die off, and men of the hills, floating down on the roaring cataracts, fill their places. On the ocean, in the warehouses, on the rostrum, in the halls of legislation, in the army or on the throne, the men of the mountains are found, rugged as their native hills, as high-minded as their mountains, and as generous as their val-

leys are deep. Don't say, then, that there is no
spirit of the hills or that there are no fairies.
Wherever the mountains are grand and the chasms
deep, wherever the waterfalls tinkle or the tor-
rent bellows, there dwell the little beings that
influence man's character. Do you say it is only
the mountains? How can cold dirt make men better
or wiser? But be it fairy or hobgoblin, dirt or
rock, men do become braver and nobler for dwelling
in the mountains.

Hence New England's position in the nation.
Hence the reason why her ideas and actions are noted
and imitated everywhere within the borders of this
nation. Oh, glorious mountains! safeguard of American freedom! go on with your divinely appointed
mission. For while you stand, and while the granite melts not or the waterfalls cease not, freedom
will be the watchword—at least in all New England!

And here, too, in East Tennessee, how the men of
the mountains fought for liberty during the War of
the Rebellion! Here they dared everything. Here
they were robbed, slandered, and murdered. But yet,
firm as these high peaks, their survivors fought
on. To be a Union man then was death. What was
that to them? The mountains taught them the value
of freedom and did not leave them nerveless in the
presence of East Tennessee hot-heads. Here, too,
came the men of the hills to conquer slavery and
rebellion. They were at the bottom of a mountain
nearly [half] a mile in height, looking up the
cliffs. The [Confederate] natives of the plains
[two brigades] were on the top [At the crest, now
called Point Park.] and glaring down. Yet the spirit
of the mountains came up and conquered. Do the boys
remember that Lookout Mountain battle of [Novem-
ber 24, 1863]? General [Joseph] Hooker, himself,
did not believe it could be done.

"Tell them to come back!" shouted the general in
command. But no notice of orders directing a retreat was taken, and onward and upward they went,
climbing precipices, rocks, and trees, swinging up
the edge of ledges, pulling one another up among
the clouds [in the "Battle Above the Clouds"], caring nothing for the hideous shell that came crashing down among the trees, until the [rocky] citadel
was taken and one more victory for freedom was re-

148

corded in the world's history.

Grand old mountain! Grand old soldiers of a grand old people! How proud of our nation and our people were we the day we visited Lookout Mountain! The changes were many which intervened between that immortal day and the May day [in 1869] when we were there. The rifle pits which Hooker's Division carried [that is, captured] and from which his forces charged up the mountain had nearly all washed away; enough was left, however, to mark the direction of the line and recall to mind the terrible events of that "great avenging day" [Alexander Pope, *The Iliad of Homer*.].

But, farther up the mountain's side, the trees and moss have grown anew, the bushes which the soldiers uprooted as they pulled themselves up have decayed and given place to others, and nothing remains to remind us of war. "Nothing!" did we say? Not so. Under a little pine tree, near the precipitous ledge which the "boys" will remember, we found a human skeleton. We were pulling ourselves along the edge of the rock, and finding our footing insecure, we seized the branch of a neighboring pine. Up it came by the roots, taking with it the thin scale of soil which covered the rock, and exposing to the sun the grinning skull of a Union soldier.

Near it was an old Springfield musket, covered with rust and broken in twain near the lock. The bayonet, so blackened and tarnished that we first took it for a stick, was thrust into the ground near the skull, and the finger bones lay about as if the soldier had clasped it when he died. A bundle, which had evidently been a knapsack, lay a few feet off and had the appearance of being in use as a bird's nest. For the little pieces of blue overcoat and threads of the gray blanket were neatly arranged in the shape of a nest. A few pieces of the spinal column lay scattered around, but otherwise the skeleton was entire. Near the spot we found a U.S. Infantry button and the soles of a pair of shoes, but nothing to identify the man who gave his life for the nation in that fearful charge. Whose son or brother he was, whose husband or father, eternity alone can tell! Yet we would not avoid the thought as we stood gazing upon the sad scene that perchance some one we personally knew might be the dearest one to this soldier of Hooker's Corps from whom his friends have never heard. "Never been heard from" is his record on the page of history. "Dead" in the records of mortals. "In Heaven," we hope, in the records of eternity. With no implements to bury them, and no soil deep enough if we had, we could not do otherwise than clamber on, leaving the bones to be ground into dust by the merciless hand of time.

Pulpit Rock [Now called Umbrella Rock.], from which Jeff Davis harangued the Confederates and near which the rebels had some of their heaviest guns, appears as familiar as an old friend and seems to smile in derision at the changeable growth and decay that has been going on around [Lookout Mountain]. The shell-split trees have recovered from their wounds; the earthworks have washed away; the hospital buildings and Negro huts are gone; yet the old rock stands on the summit like a sentinel and will stand there [Point Park. The rock still stands in the 1970's!] in the hundred years to come to tell the story of the slave-holding rebellion and the charge of the National troops. [For the origin of the phrase, "Battle Above the Clouds," and its later rejection, see J. Cutler Andrews, *The North Reports the Civil War* (Pittsburgh: U. of Pittsburgh Press, 1955), pp. 481, 725-726.]

CHATTANOOGA

We passed down the eastern slope of the great mountain to ascertain how Chattanooga appears today. The old forts, which crowned every hill around the little town, look like the Indian mounds of Illinois: no regularity, no apparent design. Little artificial hills and valleys only. Few soldiers, were it not for the everlasting hills around, which God made, would recognize the forts they garrisoned—so torn and shattered, decayed and washed are they now. A few years and even these red mounds will have disappeared and the "great railroad center" of Chattanooga will not dream of battle or siege. The town itself has not recovered from the war, that is, unless it always had a forsaken, slovenly appearance. Removing the tents, the barracks, and the stables, and filling the quartermaster's stores and the commissary warehouses with peanuts and candy, soda water and persimmon beer is a "sinking in poetry" [Alexander Pope, *Peri Bathous or Martinus Scriblerus His Treatise of the Art of Sinking in Poetry* (London: Motte, 1727).] that strikes the returner [Conwell, who had first visited there in the summer of 1864.] first as being a little ridiculous.

The old headquarters, where [George G.] Thomas, [Ulysses S.] Grant, [William T.] Sherman, and [James B.] McPherson had their quarters, still stands near the town house, so unchanged that we felt as if one of them ought to be sitting on the front porch. A new bridge has been built across the [Tennessee] river, and the old swing ferry is going to decay. Cameron Hill, with its washed earthworks, is said to be destined for the grounds and mansion of a Massachusetts man who went to Chattanooga to engage in building the new railroad line south to Charleston, S.C. Some ruins and dilapidated walls of houses destroyed during the war still remain, although many have been cleared away preparatory to reconstruction.

The old railroad depot [Union Station] still bears the marks of the soldiers' penknives, and the name of many a sentinel which wished thus to immortalize it stands out in bold relief from the soft boards on which it is carved. The short trains of half-loaded cars that now come and go form a striking contrast with the long, over-loaded trains that came and went when Sherman was marching on Atlanta. The fields around, which were covered so thick with tents when [Confederate General Braxton] Bragg threatened the town and on which have been so many brigade drills and dress parades, are now verdant with growing grain.

It was exceedingly gratifying amid the many changes that have taken place to see at least one familiar object. The national flag was there. About half way between Orchard Knob and the town and near the [Nashville &] Chattanooga Railroad stands the National Cemetery, and above it, in all its pride and glory, waves the ensign of the United States. When we visited the cemetery it was nearly dark. The flag was later hauled down, and the keeper had shut the gate,and the dew was beginning to fall. We clambered over the fence and strayed among the graves, endeavoring to find how many of the 33d Massachusetts [Regiment, Infantry] lay there. [Interred there are 13,001 soldiers, only 8,038 known.] We supposed ourself to be the only person in the grounds.

Suddenly, from a little clump of graves beyond the flag-staff a voice arose as clear and sweet as an angel's, singing the familiar words

> When we hear the music ringing
> Thro' the bright celestial dome,
> When sweet angel voices singing
> Gladly bid us welcome home
> To the land of ancient story,
> Where the spirit knows no care,
> In the land of light and glory,
> Shall we know each other there?

[Title is "Shall We Know Each Other There?" published 1862 by Horace Waters, New York, in sheet-music format.]

Had a voice from the tomb pronounced the approach of the last great day we could not have been more startled—so quiet and still had the cemetery been. For a moment we stared in the direction from which the voice proceeded, uncertain whether all the ghost stories of our youth were not coming true and hoping if it was the voice of a spirit that it would wait for us "to retreat in good order" before it resorted to any fiercer demonstration to deprive us of our wits. After a second thought, however, we concluded that it was the voice of a woman,and as some women are but our ideals of angels, it did not take much from the interest of the occasion.

Going up to the flag-staff as silently as we could,we sat down upon a mound, and when the second verse began we endeavored to chime in the bass. In that we were unkind. We ought to have known that if a woman's voice could startle us,how much more alarming would it be to a woman to hear a voice at once suggestive of the men whose graves surrounded her,singing such a song with her. But we did not stop to think. Impulse—nothing else—

was our motive. So we sang, with just such a consequence as any man of common sense might have foreseen. She had reached the chorus, in which the bass repeats the words "shall we know" while the soprano prolongs the sound of the word "know" before she seemed to discover that she was not singing alone, and, with a shriek as piercing as the song was sweet, a lady in black started from the grave of a soldier, exclaiming in hysterics, "What is that? oh! oh! oh! Don't hurt me! oh! oh! oh! My God! Oh dear, oh! dear, oh! dear, what shall I do?"

"I did not intend to frighten you. I am exceedingly sorry for it," said I, stepping out from the staff.

"Oh, sir, was it you? Did you sing?" exclaimed she, wiping her eyes with a handkerchief and uttering an hysterical laugh—half cry and half laugh —and looking wildly toward the gate.

"I do not wonder that my singing frightened you," said I, "but it is a question which of us was the most startled."

So saying, we offered to escort her home, as it was growing dark. But this she declined, saying she wished to stay awhile longer near this spot, as she "must go to-morrow," and we left her kneeling by the grave of an Ohio soldier, murmuring again the song "Shall We Know Each Other There?"

MISSIONARY RIDGE

The next day we strolled along Missionary Ridge to find such traces as might remain of that great Nov. [23-25, 1863] battle when the troops by unexampled bravery outgeneraled their own officers. But the growth of the woods and the action of the heavy rains have obliterated nearly every mark of the battle, and without a guide a stranger to the field must have great difficulty in finding the "line of battle." Occasionally a shattered tree, here and there an old shell in the thicket, and little open spots where works once stood are all that is left to tell the tale of war. All the soldiers who were buried here, both Federal and Confederate, have been taken up and removed to Chattanooga.

Near the place where Sherman's Division made the "most brilliant charge of the war," we found the picket posts, in some instances just as the soldiers left them five years ago. Some were of standing logs, one end on the ground and the other leaning against a tree, several of which were placed near enough together to protect the picket behind them while he rested his gun across the top. In other places short pieces of stone wall or a leaf-filled hole in the ground showed where some picket took measures to protect himself. For hours we traveled, clambering up rocks, over trees, and through groves, until, starting down the mountain toward Chickamauga Creek, we stopped in at a mud-chinked log hovel to rest and get out of the blistering sun.

CHATTANOOGA TO ATLANTA

We have often wondered how Xenophon's 10,000 honey-stealing bummers could manage to confiscate as much as they did in their march [about 400 B.C.] from Babylon to the Euxine [Black Sea] and that, too, in the face of strict orders from [Generals] Clearchus and Cleanor forbidding foraging. But since we have revisited the old scenes between Chattanooga and Atlanta and recalled the often-broken orders [in 1864] against straggling which were repeatedly published during that campaign, we have ceased to wonder at the impudence of the Greeks. The [retreating] Greeks had the advantage, or disadvantage, of having [Xenophon], a fighting editor from Athens, to take notes of their doings, and who wrote it up [as the *Anabasis*] after he reached his native land. [He has been called the first war correspondent.] Much has been said and written about "Sherman's bummers" while they were "marching through Georgia" [A line from Henry C. Work's lyric with that title.], yet nothing but the most meager references have ever been made in print [prior to 1869] to the devastation by the army before reaching Atlanta. [Foraging by the "bummers" is described in Andrews, p. 577-578.]

We remember [in the summer of 1864] hearing an Iowa captain give the following commands after leaving Big Shanty [Since 1870 officially called

Kennesaw but still informally "Big Shanty."]:
"Boys! I've got to fall back in the rear for half
an hour,and I don't want any of you to forget the
strict orders against foraging. So,although there
is a big pile of sweet potatoes and a dozen bee-
hives about a half a mile ahead, yet I shall expect to see every man in his place when I come back
in just three quarters of an hour from now."
When he came back every man was in his place,
hiding his smiles behind a huge potato or a great
card of crystal honey. The captain had all he
cared to eat,remarking incidentally that he was
"glad to see that the quartermaster was giving the
boys better rations." The result of this falling
to the rear and reminding the boys of the orders
whenever the officers knew of a "good haul" is more
apparent today than it was during the war. Partially destroyed villages were so soon filled with
tents; the rough barracks so soon took the place
of dwellings destroyed and were always so lively
with garrisoning soldiery,that the sad effects of
raiding were almost entirely hid. But now that the
soldiers are gone and the cities of white tents are
removed, the bare hills and ruin-marked valleys
present a ghastly and desolate aspect.
All along the [Chattanooga & Atlanta] Railroad
[through the Appalachian Mountains] from Ringgold
[southeast of Chattanooga] to Atlanta [Georgia]
black ruins,old chimneys, broken bridges, and dilapidated fences astonish the eye of the traveller.
Ruin! ruin! ruin! Some of the refugees that left
these homes in flames have returned to build another habitation, but "the last state of that man
is worse than the first" [Luke 11:26.]. The old
log houses which many occupied, with their leaky
roofs and mud-plastered walls, were bad enough,
but they were palaces beside many shanties which
now temporarily occupy their place. In the towns,
too, everything which can be used as a shelter is
appropriated,and many a white family has taken up
their abode in the hut of one of their old slaves
close beside the ghastly walls of their former mansion.
In several places a little corner in the roofless
walls of once proud mansions has been partitioned
off with slabs and logs and made to answer all the

practical purposes of a dwelling. Crops of grain in some places cover the plains [that is, fields] in their waving beauty; but all the fences,barns, Negro quarters and stables are gone. It is true that the work of rebuilding the houses, barns,and fences has begun, and before many years the effects of the war will be covered by new civil enterprises. But today the sad reminders of war are abundant. In many places the rifle pits and forts remain entire,lacking only the guns to revive the scenes of '64. Block houses partially destroyed can be seen along the route, marking the spots where were stationed the garrisons who defended Sherman's communications with Chattanooga.

Silver plate and valuables are found in Resaca nearly every day in places where the owners hid them away in time of the battle and never lived to tell where they put them. Or if they lived, the houses were burned, the private marks removed, or their memory failed to answer the demand made upon it. A nice gold watch melted into a blackened lump lay kicking about the streets of Resaca for several weeks before its value was discovered.

Kingston,at the junction [of two railroads],has a forsaken appearance since the tents of the garrison, the quartermaster's storehouses, and the sutler's shanties have disappeared. Old cars stand on a side track marked "U.S. Military R.R.," and a few of the breastworks on the hills around remain.

At Big Shanty [Station,named for railroad workers' shanties],we found nothing but the old blacksmith's shop to mark the place where such a vast army [of General William T. Sherman] encamped,and where so many poor fellow suffered and died in the [tent] hospital. [Captain Louis C. Duncan, in his article series titled "The Medical Department of the United States Army in the Civil War," (Washington: Surgeon General's Office, 1914) chap. X, pp. 10-11, calls it a "clearing hospital"which, after June 11, 1864, was brought up the railroad grade to the Big Shanty Station to receive the wounded transferred there. Reports in *Medical and Surgical History of the War of the Rebellion,* ed. U.S. Surgeon General Joseph K. Barnes(Washington: Government Printing Office, 1870), Appendix to pt. I, pp. 299-393,state that "a large field hospital, consisting of 100 tents and all the appurtenances...was following in the rear of the [advancing Union Army], at a convenient distance, keeping the line of the...railroad....This field hospital was first established at Ringgold, Ga., where it remained until May 16, 1864, when it was brought forward to Resaca in order to receive the soldiery wounded [May 13-15] in that action. It there remained until the last days of June when it was transferred to Big Shanty....The wounded from the various assaults and skirmishes in and about Kenesaw were transferred from the division hospitals to Ackworth and Big Shanty and thence by rail to Chattanooga.... The frequent changes in the positions of the troops necessitated almost a daily change in the location of these [tent] hospitals. ...The day after the battle [of Kenesaw Mountain, June 27] the wounded were all sent to the general field hospital at Big Shanty." General Sherman's headquarters were in that little village in mid-June. See also details of the army raid at Big Shanty Hotel in Andrews, pp. 559-560, 735.] We went upon the hill near the railroad cut,where [in the summer of 1864] we last saw Mother [Mary Ann] Bickerdyke, the Florence Nightingale of the West, caring for the sick in the Army-of-the-Tennessee [Field] Hospital. We found there some tent pins and the hewn tree under which so many dead were laid [out] before burial.

Then we hired a miserable mule team and started for Kenesaw Mountain. All the way for several miles the fields are cut up with entrenchments. Ton after ton of lead bullets have been exhumed from these works, and many of the people declare they should have starved had it not been for this source of income.Not a man did we meet on the road and hardly a mark of civilization was to be seen. Dreary and gloomy,Kenesaw [Now a National Battlefield Park.] stands looking down upon mile after mile of redoubts and bomb-proofs—all tenantless except by the foxes and panthers [cougars or mountain lions]. The trees, which were wounded like many of the men, have died since. On the side of Kenesaw we found the little defences raised by the pickets, while some of the trees around bore the marks of over a hundred bullets. An old gun in a

thicket and the handle of a broken sword at the
foot of a tree were all the relics of the field we
saw. The [Confederate] fort at the summit of the
mountain is still in a good state of preservation.
We stopped on the mountain but a short time and
hurried down through the earthworks and fields of
grain to the cozy little town of Marietta.
Marietta suffered terribly in the war, and its
broken fences, black house-walls, and scattered
[plank] sidewalks attest its ruin. The beautiful
shade trees and public beds of roses, the rich fruit
and cloudy grape vines are nearly all destroyed.
What is left of the town is bare and cheerless,
having the appearance of being haunted by bats and
owls rather than occupied as human dwellings. The
ruins of the Georgia Military Institute [a mile
south of the village] will soon, it is now expected,
be replaced by a building exceeding its former
grandeur. If this does occur there is a future
for Marietta yet.
Then we proceeded by rail to Atlanta. Here much
has been done to cover the marks of war. Thrift
and enterprise show on every side and in a few
years Atlanta must soon far outdo her former self.
[The city had been the State Capital less than a
year.] Many building spots made vacant by the war
still remain unoccupied, and a few shell-torn houses
remain unrepaired. But the greater portion of the
city is looking fresh and cheerful. Farmers have
leveled a large portion of the earthworks around
the city, yet sufficient remain to show the importance which [Confederate General John B.] Hood
and [General Joseph E.] Johnston placed upon the
defence of the city.
From Atlanta we rode out through the cotton fields
to the battle-field of Atlanta and the Chattahoo-
chee River. But the change was so great which
marks the transformation from earthworks, tents,
signal and picket posts to fields of cotton and
sweet potatoes that had we trusted to ourself we
would have failed in finding any of the localities
of which we were in search. But with the aid of a
[former] Confederate soldier we wound through the
grain and cotton fields and crossing Peach Tree
Creek were soon on the spot where fell [Union]
General [James B.] McPherson [on July 28, 1864].

The redoubts were crumbling down, the logs which composed them were going fast to decay,and little trees and bushes had almost overgrown the ditches where [Confederate General William J. Hardee]made his fearful [cavalry] charge on the morning of the 22d of July. Yet we found the open spot, the old stump, and the large tree which mark the place where McPherson fell [shot by rebel riflemen]. [A cannon-shaped memorial now stands at McPherson and Monument Avenues.]

On our return from Atlanta [by rail] we visited Acworth, Rome, Allatoona, Adairsville, Dalton, Buzzard's Roost, and Tunnel Hill. But they were so shattered and broken, so desolate and lonely that we were glad when we were back at Chattanooga. Nothing but the hills and valleys appear as they did when the army was there. Many of the inhabitants have never returned, and those who have come back, with very few exceptions, have no energy to resuscitate the fields that lay in the track of Sherman's blighting army.

KNOXVILLE

In swinging around the great circle occupied by the Union armies during the war with rebellion,we have seen much that was interesting both in nature and in art and have gained a higher opinion of the natural advantages of our great land than we ever had before. But the localities which left the best impressions, and in which we would prefer to live if ever we should make the Sunny South our home, lie in and around Knoxville,the metropolis of East Tennessee. The rolling hills and sloping valleys, the forests and rivers are all so beautiful in themselves and so pleasingly combined that the traveller, tired and worn with a monotonous journey over the plains of the Gulf States, sits down at Knoxville with a deep sigh of relief and says, "Here I can rest."

As we stood upon the summit occupied by the ruins of Fort Sanders and surveyed the wonderful beauty of our natural surroundings,noting the brilliancy of the Holston River,the green fields on the mountain side and the quiet little city partially hid by the hills,we were almost persuaded that it was

the most beautiful spot we ever saw. Far away to
the east the ranges of the Blue Ridge and Alleghany
arose one beyond the other, dark, mysterious, and
gloomy;while far beyond them appeared the ponderous peaks [Pisgah, Mitchell, Bald, and Roan] of
another mountain range barely outlined against the
ethereal blue. In the west and south other mountains [the Cumberlands] of less magnitude arose in
silent grandeur, and the valley seemed to be enclosed by these mighty monuments of the Almighty's
power.
A valley of cultivated hills is the best defini-
tion we can give of the locality. It is beautiful
and grand even in the vicinity of the city; but
the sublimity of the dark mountains in the distance is too profound to be described by us or to
be understood by any who have not seen the Alps
[Conwell, while on a tour of Europe, had visited
the Alps two years before.]or the Rocky Mountains.
Suffice it to say that while looking at them the
beholder senses how insignificant and weak is man
and how great and mighty is God!
We question, however,whether the men who fought
on that memorable day at Fort Sanders, when [Con-
federate General James] Longstreet [in 1863] besieged the city,took much notice then whether the
mountains were grand or not. To defeat Longstreet
and get some hard tack were thoughts of too much
importance to allow their minds to seek such triv-
ial affairs as the mountain scenery, and we ask
pardon of the 29th and 36th Massachusetts for men-
tioning the scenery before we referred to the battle.
Knoxville had been the scene of much social and
domestic strife through the first years of the war.
Union men and rebels had been hanged and imprisoned by their neighbors, the party temporarily in
power always attempting to outdo their predecessors in vengeance on their enemies. [William G.]
Brownlow ["the fighting parson" and governor of
Tennessee, 1865-1869] and [Andrew] Johnson [suc-
cessor to Lincoln as president] had thundered away
at the rebellion [and slave-holding aristocracy],
cursing the rebels and being cursed by them until
Confederate General[Simon B.]Buckner occupied the
city of Knoxville [to September,1863] for the pur-

pose of rooting out [what he called] the "Union
sentiment of East Tennessee." Buckner ruled awhile
with a high hand. Whoso hated rebellion hated the
Confederacy. Whoso hated the Confederacy was an
outlaw and a traitor. Thus reasoned Buckner, and
such was the theory he put into practice.

After him came [Major General Ambrose E.] Burnside (in a double sense), and Buckner thought he
had seen enough of the old Ninth Corps and "spec-
fully took his leabins." But when a part of the
Ninth Corps were gone and the garrison small (as
Grant must fight soon at Mission [ary] Ridge),
[General] Longstreet came in his might to capture
Burnside and his little garrison. Once, twice,
thrice he tried to storm the defenses of Knoxville,
and being each time terribly defeated, he concluded that it was "not a part of his plan to take
it by assault."

Then came the siege [November to December,1863],
then the hard picket duty, then the scarcity of
food,then the suffering,the scenes of starvation,
then the death-beds, and lastly the silent funeral processions. How many Massachusetts boys felt
thankful, when they saw the emaciated citizens
hunting for food, that they still had "one hard-
tack left." How well do they remember that dark
and stormy night when Longstreet's men were active
near Armstrong's white house over on the hill [less
than a mile from Fort Sanders] and when the boys
lay on their arms,starting at every little sound,
thinking that it might be the approach of the enemy. And then the next morning at 6 o'clock! Ah!
that was a great day in the history of the 29th
[Massachusetts]. They cannot forget how they stood
behind the works in Fort Sanders and saw the long
gray line of the enemy start out of the trees far
in the distance.

How the rebel shot and shell scattered the dirt
in the faces of the little [Union] garrison! Whizzing, hissing, shrieking, bursting, thundering—
the artillery rained a terrible storm upon them,
while the gray line came nearer, and nearer, and
nearer. How the hills rang with the yell! On they
came like the demons of hell. Over the knolls,into
the ravines,around the stumps, and over the fall-
en trees, until within musket range,when, lo, the

whole line went down together. Entangled in the
network of [telegraph] wires spread from stump to
stump to catch their unwary feet, they squirmed
and yelled,rolled on the ground, extricated themselves with difficulty;and while many fled,a part
came on. Up the ditch they came. But the smoke
of the musketry blazing in their faces hid them
from view. Down into the ditch and upon the parapet!
"They must be in the fort!" says Burnside.
Oh no! not yet, not yet! The firing goes on!
The flag is up and the yells continue! Suddenly a
loud volley that shook the hills echoed down the
valley;the smoke began to clear away; loud shouts
of victory arose;and the field was won. All along
the ditch,beside the bastions and among the stumps
that dotted the field in front lay 400 dead soldiers—brave men if they were rebels—while in the
ditch with their guns thrown down and their hands
thrown up stood 300 of the enemy who dare not attempt to flee.

This was the scene described to us by a Massachusetts soldier who showed us the spot, and we
smiled amidst his glowing description to hear him
remark that Longstreet "felt like as if he wanted
ter go home." However he may have felt, home he
did go. The siege was at once abandoned,and hard-
tack and salt horse were again as plentiful as ever.
The marks of that fight are still visible. The
stumps which covered the sides of the hill upon
which stood Fort Sanders are filled with bullets,
and pieces of shell can be picked up in every direction. The fort itself has gone to ruin fast,
and when we were there the action of the rain had
worn down the embankments and nearly filled the
ditches. The old quartermaster's storehouses and
the garrison huts had all disappeared, and only
their foundations could be shown us. Long we could
have stood at Fort Sanders contemplating the scene
and picturing to ourself the appearance of the hills
in the dark days of '64. But as our limited time
could be much better spent than in musing, we acted
on the hint of our guide and turned toward the
city.

The County Jail in which [Parson] Brownlow and
his friends were confined, when many were taken

out and hanged, while all were threatened daily
with a like fate, stands as grim and uninviting as
ever. The cell in which he stood and prayed, when
there was not room enough for all to kneel down,
is as dirty now as when he occupied it. The coarse,
rusty grates through which came the light and
through which the old patriot and hero gazed hour
after hour, still darken the little window of the
cell.

The iron cages in which Union men were incar-
cerated only to be taken out and left hanging to
a tree for the insults of soldiery and the food of
ravens are still held in their places by the solid
masonry. Criminals now have the honor of standing
where Brownlow stood and of sleeping where martyrs have slept. From the jail we passed the house
of the Hon. Horace Maynard [then United States representative from Tennessee], who shared with Brownlow [the opposition to secession] the dangers and
trials of those bloody days. The buildings looked
dilapidated and worn, and we should have joined
with his enemies in accusing him of neglecting his
home had we not recollected that his house was
General Buckner's headquarters, and that everything
which could, without inconveniencing the usurper,
be destroyed, was broken and scattered by the rebel soldiers. Nearly opposite was the residence of
Hon. Thomas A. R. Nelson, who defended Andrew Johnson in the great impeachment farce [last year].

We could not leave Knoxville without seeing Parson Brownlow whose name and deeds have become so
famous, and so we called at his house. His dwelling is a simple wooden structure in the poorer
part of the city and would hardly be selected by
a stranger as the home of a U.S. senator. We found
the parson [who had recently been elected senator]
sitting in an easy chair, somewhat improved in
health since the time we had last heard from him.
But his face was thin and pale, his eyes sunken,
and his [palsied] hands shook at a fearful rate
whenever he moved them from a reclining position.
[He was then 64.] His voice was too weak for much
conversation, so we stopped but a few minutes with
him. He seemed cheerful and thinks he will recover, but to us it seemed a hopeless case. [But
he lived until 1877, having served in the Senate

six years.] We learned that he was able to ride out once in a great while,and when he did so,even his old enemies treated him with profound respect. The Knoxville *Whig* [newspaper] which made such a muss with rebellion when the war broke out,and for editing which [1849-1861] the rebels can never forgive Brownlow or his son, has passed into the hands of another Methodist minister,a counterpart of Brownlow, and has been removed from the low wooden building in which it was published to a fine brick building on the principal business street of the city. Thus the patriotism of the few who were brave enough to peril their lives for a patriotic principle has been repaid. Heap the honors upon them! They cannot be too well rewarded.

But it would be the height of folly to suppose that the rebellious,slavery-loving spirit is dead in East Tennessee or that the persecution of Brownlow and his class of men is at an end. Ah no! Feuds still exist and threats of vengeance and death are still made. The Methodist [Episcopal] Church North and the Methodist [Episcopal] Church South have nothing to do with each other, and the members of one will not speak to the members of the other. But behind their backs each revileth the other in a most un-Christian manner. They believe in separating the sheep from the goats but disagree as to which church contains the goats.

God bless the Methodists for their zeal in patriotism as well as in religion. They were a mighty power in the North during the war, a Methodist prayer and a Methodist bayonet being always pointed. It meant something! But it will be a long time,we fear,before a reconciliation between the Methodist Church North and the Methodist Church South can be brought about. [A reunion was realized seventy years later—in 1939.]

We would not be understood, however,as claiming that the South is not fast becoming reconciled to the new order of things, or that, as a general thing,it is unsafe in the South for Northern men. But we do mean to say that rebellion is not dead yet, and [now in 1869] thousands are waiting and hoping that a foreign war may come and they yet get assistance to drive the carpet-baggers back to the North and see Jeff Davis reinstated. But the old flag is there, waving proudly as of old,while

beneath it there sleep in Knoxville 6,000 Union
dead.

Wave on,glad emblem of freedom! Sleep on,brave
patriot dead! Neither shall die in the hearts of
men, though rebellion may rage and traitors may
thrive for a time. An eternal principle ye repre-
sent which God will not let die. The old camp
ground on which ye lie may be forgotten. The proud
flag may be tattered and soiled; the men who knew
them may pass away, and the battle-field,and even
the city itself,fade from sight. But on that first
eternal day this army of martyrs shall arise to
proclaim the success of that holy principle of
freedom for which they died.

GREENVILLE

But we linger too long at Knoxville and must hurry on to Greenville [Tennessee] where we saw Andy
Johnson in bold array. The low building in which
he was a tailor, and the small office in which he
was a lawyer, and the white wood house of modest
proportion in which he is the ex-President of the
United States were pointed out to us with pride by
one of his townsmen, a mule driver. Mr. Johnson
treated us cordially,said it was a necessary evil
following a great man that everybody thought it an
honor to speak to him and bother him for opinions.
We didn't "bother him for opinions," nor would we
under any circumstances, any more than we would
spend our valuable time chasing a gander to hear
him squawk. Mr. Johnson has purchased a big farm,
about twenty miles from Greenville, on which is a
mill that he proposes to have "support him for the
Senate." [He was elected and served a short term.
He is buried at Greenville in Andrew Johnson National Cemetery.]

Next we journeyed from Greenville over the
mountains and into the beautiful valleys of Virginia. All along the route, however, from Knoxville [between the Blue Ridge and Alleghany Moun-
tains] to the Shenandoah Valley we saw rifle pits
and stockades, with here and there a shot-scarred
tree; but who fired the shot or who was killed,
neither history nor our recollection can tell us.
The raiders and scouting parties left scarce a spot

untouched, as the ruins of dwellings and fences show.

We could not fail to notice the difference between those farms cultivated by the industry and skill of Yankees who have settled in many places along the road, and the tracts of land not cultivated but neglected by the native owners. On one side of the turnpike is the new house of a Vermonter. The dwelling is well built and after a neat design. The barn is tight and capacious. There are walks in the securely fenced front yard and newly set out shade trees and long beds of flowers with a profusion of rose bushes. Behind the house is a thrifty orchard growing from a beautiful lawn of dark rank clover, while as far as we can see the land is under cultivation and the crops of corn, wheat, and potatoes look beautiful and promising. The owner himself is at work with his hired help, weeding at the various beds of vegetables which adorn and utilize his large garden. The clothes on the line speak a good word for the neat housewife, while the children, as they start off for school loaded down with arithmetic and geography [books], are the pictures of health, beauty, and happiness. The traveller gazes on the place with a feeling of pride and satisfaction and is sensibly refreshed by the scene.

But on the opposite side of the road is the home of a Virginian. The old brown structure in which the "lord of creation" [Robert Burns, "The Twa Dogs."] lives is rickety and dilapidated. The shingles are playing curious antics on the roof; the chimneys on the outside of the house have lost many bricks and look as if they were saying a last farewell to the wooden structure to which they have been so long united. The front door is broken and patched. The low windows are spotted with old hats and papers stuffed into keep out the wet and cold. The yard in the immediate vicinity of the door is strewn with every conceivable kind of rubbish, and the visitor is obliged to go around a dead-sea of slops and a half-dozen starved and wallowing pigs to reach the steps. A little way down from the house is an excuse for a garden, but the few sweet potatoes and onions which are supposed to grow there are completely hid in the famished weeds.

The land under cultivation—but a small part of his barren, unproductive waste—has only been scratched two inches deep with a wooden plough,and the crops look sickly and small. This "constant-taking-off-and-never-putting-on" principle has exhausted the land; the owner, having lost his slaves, does not possess the energy to recall its fertility,and sand hills and little clumps of pine trees will be his principal crop. No barns, no stables,no fences,no orchards—perhaps one or two old, half-dead peach trees—he lives on from day to day, doing as little as he can, allowing his children to hunt and fish, while their nakedness is scarce covered with rags,refusing to associate with the "laboring Yankee," and cursing his prosperous neighbor for invading the "sacred soil." Laziness and unthriftiness, pride and foolishness were his birthright,and lazy and unthrifty he will die. Looking down from his high station, in rags, dirt, ignorance, and idleness, upon the man whose land under his own tilling is blooming with fertility, he says, as we have heard him say many times, "I'm a Virginian, by ——; I'm a man of honor; I descended from noble stock that knew no labor; I'm a native Virginian; shall I be seen associating with a common laborer? Not by a —— sight."

LYNCHBURG

While we were at Lynchburg [about twenty miles west of Appomattox],rebel General Jubal [A.] Early was then "acting lion of the day." He walked about the streets with all the airs of a conqueror [He had just returned from self-imposed exile in Mexico, Cuba, and Canada.] and refused a public dinner offered him by the citizens on the ground that it would be unpleasant "for some men" to hear what he should say of The Lost Cause on an occasion like that. [A practising lawyer, he remained bitter against the North,a permanent rebel.] When we saw him he was walking up the street with an elderly appearing gentleman, with whom he was in earnest conversation. At a corner they met a colored man who was hurrying toward the market with a basket of vegetables. General Early glanced at the man and, with a ceremonious bow, said, "Good morning, John," and passed on. The darkey suddenly came to a stop, put his basket on a doorstep, and brought his arms akimbo, all the while eyeing the receding couple with an expression of profound surprise. "Lor!" said he, after gazing after them a moment. "Who dat man? He look like a man ob de Souf. An he says good mornin' to dis nigger! Gosh! he must be somebody, for dis nigger nebber seed him afore. Oh, yah, yah, yah, I hab him now; I beleebe he's some ole feller what dun know de Federacy is done gone and busted and de cullud folks is theirseves now."

CULPEPPER COURT HOUSE

Back in "Ole Virginny!" Where the yellow mud sticks and slops, and where the sleepy enterprise of the people cannot cover the fearful marks of war. But human strife has not robbed Virginia of her natural beauties, and although fences be gone, the houses broken and torn, and the fields covered with falling earthworks, yet the hills and plains, rivers and ravines are as picturesque and romantic as ever.

Especially is this the case around Culpepper Court House. The rolling prairies which stretch far away from the little town are checkered with grain fields that bow before the wind as if answering to the hope of their owners—that they might come to a pleasant and bountiful harvest. Rich shade trees dot the landscape with a darker green, and the little stream that flows [eastward into] the Rappahannock [River] twinkles and glistens through the meadows as cheerful as though there had been no war—more mildly grand than they would have been if fences had not been destroyed, and more fertile for graves that lie beneath them. Hills and valleys smile in derision at the very mention of war.

In no locality that we have seen have the marks of war been more effectually obliterated than around Culpepper. There are, it is true, many little openings in the wheatfields and grey spots in the cornfields, which the very close observer recognizes as the uncultivated sandhills that arose during the war; while broken trees, with here and there the blackened remains of fence posts, hint, also, at the ravages of war. But while the harvest is blooming, the casual observer sees them not and thinks it strange that the land about Culpepper should be so soon recovered, while other more accessible parts of Virginia remain a desert. But more than that which is lost in the fields is made up in the town. Some houses have been constructed since the war, and some repaired.

"But the trail of the Serpent is over them all!" [Thomas Moore, "Lalla Rookh."]

A feeling of gloom seizes upon the traveller who treads its streets, which neither the genial faces of a few speculating Yankees from New England nor the passing of the blustering locomotive can dispel. He looks up involuntarily at noonday and wonders if it is not going to rain. It seems as if there must be a cloud somewhere, even if he cannot see it. The old blacksmith shop where army horses were shod was shut; the grand old courthouse walls were naked and hollow when we were there; and the sight of a neat little cottage near it seemed like a mockery. The people too are as gloomy as the town—so it seemed to us. They were cheerful enough after [the Battles of] Bull Run [in the summers of 1861 and 1862] and came out in holiday attire, expressing a determination to "dress well if they didn't lay up a cent" when celebrating such victories! But to-day, those who wore new clothes then appear ragged and dirty.

If there had been no battles hereabouts—no Cedar Mountain [August 9, 1862], Brandy Station [June 9, 1863], Mine Run and Germania Ford [May-June, 1864], Kelly's Ford [March 17, 1863], nor Rappahannock [River]—this town would be dull enough for a correspondent; and as it is, the best thing we can say of its present appearance is that there was nothing more in the town to tempt a soldier to "go through it" than there was in '64.

BRANDY STATION

We could not muster the courage to stop over night at Brandy Station [on the Orange & Alexan-

dria Railroad], for judging from what we could see
from the cars we would have been much less "warmly
received" than were some of our acquaintances under
[General George G.] Meade [in the great cavalry
battle against Confederate General "Jeb" Stuart]
on [June 9], 1863. There was one house in sight,
besides the shed at the station, and both of them
appeared untenanted. A few logs were left standing of a stockade near the depot, and a short line
of low breastworks. Out on a little hill were the
remains of what was once a redoubt; but the land
about it and everywhere within sight, in fact, appeared desolate and wild.

"I would recommend," said a travelling companion [in the railway coach], "that when your folks
come down from the North to settle this land that
they bring fencing stuff enough to make up for the
rails and posts which they [the Union soldiers]
burned when they were here."

"Did they really burn fences?" said we with
feigned surprise.

"Lord bless you, yes," said he. "I lived just a
little way from Cedar Mountain [south of Culpepper],
and one night the Yankee army came along and camped
just a little way from my house; and the very first
thing they did was to steal all my field fence
rails and even the pickets on my yard fence. They
got a big bundle on their shoulders, and then they
would shout, 'Co. A, 39th!' or whatever their regiment was; and whenever they got an answer through
the darkness, off they would go toward their camps
with my fencing stuff. After they had torn down
everything moveable, and I had seen them from my
windows, several came and said 'General [Joseph]
Wheeler' [Confederate cavalry leader] wanted the
house for brigade headquarters. I told them I was
too happy to accommodate him—for I couldn't help
myself, you know—and offered to lend them some of
my fence rails to build their camp fires. They
took it as a joke, and went away and informed 'General Wheeler' that the house was ready."

"Have you ever built your fences again?" enquired
we.

"Oh! no. I've been trying this two years to sell
my farm to Northern emigrants, but some of the very
soldiers who toasted their shins by a fire made of

my rails have refused to buy my farm, because it wasn't fenced! cuss 'em!"

The noise of the rattling [O&A] train, as we lumbered away from Brandy Station, cut short our discussion on the [fence] rail question and left us more at liberty to gaze out the window. Both sides of the road, from the Station to Manassas Junction, the fragments of block houses, broken portions of fortifications, and small sections of stockade fences were pointed out as the forts upon the strength of which the fate of the nation, a few years ago, depended. But they are fast losing their identity, and in a few years more it will be said of them, as of the men who fought there, "The place that knew them shall know them no more" [Variation of Job 7:10.].

MANASSAS JUNCTION

The little village at Manassas Junction is called a city but it has no blocks and no sidewalks. It is much easier to tell what it does possess than what it does not, so we will change our phraseology and say that it contains one hotel (i.e., a place where folks are taken in for the night), one livery stable with two army horses and a mule, and a grocery where molasses and gin are drawn mixed [that is, the same container is used] whenever either is ordered. How much of a place it might have been before the war we do not know; but now, as a darkey expressed it, "It be forsook by ebryting 'cept de berry debbil."

Hundreds of visitors, however, stop over at this place to visit the battle-field of Bull Run; and it would seem as if so much transient patronage, which is increasing every year, would give to the place an air of enterprise and prosperity. But such is by no means the case. In every direction from the depot can be seen lines of earthworks and trenches with here and there a fort, lacking only the guns to revive entire the scene in war time. A few have been leveled by the farmers and by Negroes searching for lead. But the greater part of the works remain as they were left, and the returning soldier can easily find the "old camp ground" or the redoubt in which he was stationed.

Probably no field in the South is more interesting to either soldier or civilian than the battlefield of Bull Run. Other fields have been so changed by cultivation or present such a different appearance when the army, with its wagons, tents, and smoke is gone, that even the generals are unable to recognize them. But Bull Run has changed little. The same old trees, clumps of bushes, deep ravines, sloping hills, and muddy bottoms are there to-day which were there when the first Massachusetts and the Third Michigan [infantry regiments] went down into the bottom to begin the First Battle of Bull Run [on July 21, 1861]. The old chimneys and broken trees, together with the monuments on the field and at [nearby] Groveton, give the same aspect to the field which it wore during the later days of the war. The old forts, from Union Mills and McLean's Ford to the dilapidated stone bridge, that were erected in piecemeal after the first battle are nearly as the soldiers left them. At Blackburn's Ford there are traces of some kind of stockade, but it could not have been used during the war. A few patches of wheat, corn, or potatoes are seen here and there, but they are not sufficiently extensive to take away the feeling of desolation which seizes the visitor as he looks over the landscape.

GROVETON

Groveton, now, as during the war, is but a collection of a half dozen ruined houses in which reside equally ruinous-looking people. One of the latter, however, points out to visitors the old farm which belonged to [Wilmer] McLean, in whose house [at Appomattox Court House] later in the war Grant and Lee signed the terms of surrender. McLean thought his house at Bull Run too near the Yankees and moved to Appomattox, declaring that he was going to settle where the Yankees could never again come to disturb him. But, as his experience shows, it is uncertain when you part with a Yankee how soon he may again appear. He is sure to visit those places where he is the least expected.

Between Groveton and Cub Run the woods are severely shattered, showing yet the marks of that

day, eight years ago. But the scenery for miles
around is but a constantly recurring picture of
broken trees,old chimneys,mud-chinked cabins, bad
roads, and pieces of earthworks. A stranger to
the place and its history would know at once that
it had been the arena of a terrible battle. Especially is this the case on the field of the Second Battle [fought August 29-30, 1862], where the
earthworks so hastily constructed are so nearly
entire.

CENTREVILLE

At Centreville there has been erected a new
church, about 20 by 30 [feet], for the accommoda-
tion of those who should attend church on Sunday.
If it had been built no larger than necessary to
accommodate those who attended when we were in town,
2 x 6 would have answered every purpose. How they
managed to raise $200, even for a church, was a
mystery to us when we noticed the ash-covered foundations, the bare frames, and lone chimneys of
dwellings and the rickety state of the few which
remained. The fortifications on the hill behind
the town seem to have been left entire because
there was no one to dig them down or cultivate the
land when they were down.

At an old one-story house we managed to get some
corn for our horses and some fried eggs and bread
for our dinner. Lounging about the door were three
or four young men who,soon after the meal was finished, fell into conversation with "Scott" and
"Burritt" [our two rented horses],who accompanied
us from Washington. The youths had been in the
Southern army and and served under [General]"Stonewall" Jackson. They all seemed to regard the devastation around with perfect indifference,and one
of them [said he] thought that the possession of a
harness like those he saw on the livery horses with
us would make him perfectly happy. They evidently were a little sorry that the Yankees were not
defeated in the end, but acted as though they did
not "care a fig" [Edward Lear, "The Jumblies."] for
Jeff Davis or any other man.

GERMANTOWN

On our return [toward Washington] we stopped at Germantown, which consists of one house at the cross-roads [of Warrenton and Little River turn-pikes]. This house is a shanty of logs and is now used as a barn. How a house at these cross-roads could have acquired such a high-sounding title as "Germantown" or how a barn could sustain the dignity of such a name was a matter of no little wonder. In the history of the war which will be handed down to coming generations, Germantown will be one of the most important towns in the Union. As a strategic point previous to the Battle of Bull Run it was an important place, and there may then have been more buildings. But to-day its name is all there is of interest or consequence about it. It is by far the smallest "town" we have seen in the South, although we have seen them composed of a house, barn, and pigsty, while "cities" might have three houses, without barns or pigsties.

FAIRFAX COURT HOUSE

An hour's drive over a smooth turnpike, upon which (if we do not exaggerate) toll was collected every three-quarters of a mile, we came to Fairfax Court House. This is a cosy, shady, little town on a slightly elevated plateau and has resumed in a measure the cheerful appearance it wore previous to the war. The old court house, a capacious hotel, and a few residences of wealthy planters remain, and in nearly every case they have been repaired and repainted since the war. Near by are broad fields of grain and rich meadows—but scarcely anything which could be called "marks of the war." On the eastern slope of the hill, however, is the "Memorial Cemetery," in which are buried a few thousand Confederate soldiers. It would seem, judging by the fences and mounds, that considerable money was spent in its construction, but the appearance of the weeds and falling head-boards showed great neglect since the work of construction ceased.

WINCHESTER

All the way up the beautiful Shenandoah Valley we had noted the change which the incoming Yankees have wrought in the appearance of the fields, and when we reached Winchester [Virginia] we were convinced that before many years the Yankees will possess the whole of this lovely valley. When we had looked about the city, visited [Union General Philip H.] Sheridan's old quarters, the National and the Confederate cemeteries (which stand side by side),and the forts on the high ground west of the city, we inquired the distance to the battleground where Sheridan won the great Battle of Winchester [September 19, 1864, against forces of Confederate General Early] and at last found Opequon Ford on the Berryville turnpike where Sheridan crossed. Fences have been built, the land ploughed up, and thousands of acres covered with waving grain border on the highway where during the war were trees or uncultivated pasture land.

We returned to Winchester feeling an uncertainty as to the exact location of that triple battle [Third Battle of Winchester], although we knew we must have passed over it. Soldiers who fought there have told us since that they have tried to find their old place upon the plain but in each instance failed. All traces have been obliterated of one of the greatest battles the world ever saw. [Union casualties were 5,000 and Confederate, 4,600.]

From Winchester we went to Fisher's Hill, where the Federal troops [on September 22, 1864] once won a victory and once [in 1862] suffered an inglorious defeat. The earthworks were still visible although the rain and the hand of the farmer are still bringing them down to the common level. Here are many Confederate dead as yet undiscovered or at least untouched by the Memorial Association which established the Confederate Cemetery at Winchester.

At [nearby] Strasburg, where our [Union] troops were so disastrously routed [by Early's army]during the absence of Sheridan [On October 19, 1864, he was in Washington for a military conference.] there are still traces of the terrible conflict, and haversacks, canteens, cartridge boxes, pieces of clothing, and shot and shell can be found in great quantities. But the dead, who were thrown into the trenches like hogs and covered with a few inches of dirt, have all been removed to the National Cemetery, and next Saturday (the 29th) their graves will be covered with flowers. [The dead there total 4,480—2,382 unknown.]

At Cedar Creek, where the "little General" [Sheridan—returning to battle] turned a disgraceful rout into a [Union] victory and where he annihilated forever Early's army, we found the earthworks still entire. The beautiful stream flowed on as quietly and sweetly through the rich meadows as though it had never seen war or been colored with blood. We sat down upon its banks and recalled the accounts we had heard of the battle, felt like hurrahing for the brave little General, and repeated these lines of [Thomas B. Read's poem] "Sheridan's Ride":

> Up from the South, at break of day,
> Bringing to Winchester fresh dismay,
> The affrighted air with a shudder bore,
> Like a herald in haste, to the chieftain's door,
> The terrible grumble, and rumble, and roar,
> Telling the battle was on once more,
> And Sheridan twenty miles away.
>
> And wider still those billows of war
> Thundered along the horizon's bar;
> And louder yet into Winchester rolled
> The roar of that red sea uncontrolled,
> Making the blood of the listener cold,
> As he thought of the stake in that fiery fray,
> And Sheridan twenty miles away.
>
> Hurrah! hurrah for Sheridan!
> Hurrah! for horse and man!
> And when their statues are placed on high,
> Under the dome of the Union sky—
> The American soldier's Temple of Fame—
> There, with the glorious general's name,
> Be it said, in letters both bold and bright,
> "Here is the steed that saved the day
> By carrying Sheridan into the fight,
> From Winchester, twenty miles away!"

HARPER'S FERRY

Then we took the cars [at Winchester] for Harper's Ferry [West Virginia]. No other place have we found, in any part of the South, so alive with interesting associations! Here it was [at the junction of the Potomac and Shenandoah rivers] that the great conflict began—the war for freedom. Here [at Harper's Ferry] that insane old man —the representative, nevertheless, of a great idea and the humble instrument in the hands of God for the performance of a great work—[abolitionist] John Brown, first opened the war with slavery. Here, with his little band [October 16, 1859], he captured the armories and fortified himself in the engine house. From this place he was taken to Charlestown, twelve miles away, tried, and hanged [December 2, 1859].

Here, too, the second act of the great tragedy was performed. Here Lieutenant [Roger] Jones, when attacked by the Virginia Militia [on April 18, 1861], set all the armory buildings on fire and blew up the [Federal] Arsenal, preventing the rebels from getting the arms and saved Washington. Here [Union] General [Robert] Patterson came [June 15, 1861] and drove [Confederate General] Joseph E. Johnston from the cragged mountain opposite, called Maryland Heights. Here Major [J. Parker] Gould of the 13th Massachusetts began the fight of Camp Heights. Here it was that General [Nathaniel P.] Banks began his campaign against [General Thomas J.] "Stonewall" Jackson. Here it was that that inefficient, cowardly Colonel [Dixon S.] Miles [Union commander] allowed himself [and 11,000 troops in September, 1862] to be entrapped by [General] Lee at the first [Confederate] invasion of Maryland. Here it was that McClellan's army lay idle after the Battle of Antietam while he "had some correspondence with Washington." Oh! that he had moved forward then! To this place withdrew [Union General Robert H.] Milroy from Winchester [in 1863] when Lee came to make a second invasion of Maryland. And here it was that the gallant [Union] General [William H.] French posted himself in Lee's rear after the Battle of Gettysburg and held the heights.

No part of our long journey through the South have we enjoyed like this visit at Harper's Ferry. We ran about from canal to railroad, barracks to hotel, from one ghastly ruin to another, and from hill to hill to see the places where such stirring events occurred. On Loudoun Heights [on the south side] we stood and thought of General [George] Washington, who once purchased the whole tract of land about Harper's Ferry. On Camp Heights we gazed at the old ruined walls of "headquarters" and recalled the history of the generals who had made it their abode. In the shot-riddled ruins that once heard the sound of prayer and of preaching we stared at the black ceiling and crumbling walls, wondering where the minister and congregation had gone. In the shattered and desolate ruins of the armory buildings we stood and pondered on the time when they were full of workmen with whom the proud Virginians would hold no intercourse.

In the little engine house, still kept as a guard house or jail by the town authorities and military, we looked at the port-holes which John Brown and his men made with their pikes and laughed in spite of ourselves to think how he had put the "raw militia" of chivalrous Virginia to flight by pointing a single musket at them. In the dismantled mills, whose walls threatened to cave in upon us, we hunted for pieces of shot and shell and regretted that such water-power and such building material should lie idle for the need of sufficient enterprise to put them to practical use.

On the magnificent iron bridge which crosses the confluence of the Shenandoah and the Potomac in the village, we walked to and fro, dreaming of the scene when the wooden bridge, its predecessor, was covered with flame and smoke. We stood on the railway and sighed for the friends of those who had fallen while tearing up the track or defending it from the foe. On that magnificent spot, far, far above the Potomac—up in the very clouds—on Maryland Heights [on the northern side of the river], we stood and gazed down upon the village and the diminutive-appearing men in the streets, imagining the effect of a few hundred-pound shot. In the old fort on the highest point we picked up pieces of old iron and tossed them against the dilapidated wall,wondering whose hands grasped them last.

Along the ridge down to the lower hills we strayed, musing upon the time when Colonel Miles threw his cannon down this rugged steep [before he surrendered his brigade]. Over the fortifications,along the hills, out to "John Brown's church" where he used to preach, out to his farm house where he lived and pretended to make mining tools, down to the canal,across again to Harper's Ferry we went. Dreary and deserted, surrounded by piles of ruins that remind one of the remains of ancient cities, situated in so narrow a valley that the sun reaches it near mid-day, Harper's Ferry is a lonesome, unthrifty place, yet there are many Yankees there from Massachusetts and Vermont who propose to build up the town. We hope they may, but we will confess to a feeling of relief when we left Harper's Ferry behind us and rode over the mountains toward Antietam [Battlefield].

SHARPSBURG

The town of Sharpsburg, Maryland, in and about which was fought [September 16-17, 1862] the Battle of Antietam and after which it would have been more appropriate to have named the fight, is the same quiet, modest little town that it was during the war. Several new houses have been built, and one is a capacious school building. The shot holes in the roofs and gables of the houses in many places remain to show the stranger the direction in which the battle [between armies of Generals McClellan and Lee] raged. Everything about the town has an air of enterprise and neatness. The blacksmith's shop and the carriage maker's establishment are surrounded by little piles of old shot, shell, gun barrels, bayonets, and bullets which enterprising boys have gathered from the battle-field. [More than 23,000 men were killed or wounded in the battle,called the bloodiest day in the Civil War. The struggle halted Lee's first invasion of the North.]

The occupants of Sharpsburg have changed but little since the battle and every one we met had a story to tell as to how they felt when [Union

General Joseph] Hooker advanced near [the] Dunker [or Dunkard] Church and [General Ambrose] Burnside charged up the hill from the stone bridge over Antietam Creek. Some fled, but, for the most part hid themselves in coal bins and dark corners of their rocky cellars, expecting, notwithstanding their precaution, to be cut into little bits by the shell which riddled the houses over their heads.

The marks of battle along the Hagerstown Road are still visible, although Time's effacing fingers have been actively at work. The rail fences beside the road in front of Hooker's position are still standing and so bullet-riddled that in some places the chestnut rails scarce hold together. The woods in and around the old church, and along back of the Hagerstown Road, are broken and torn, not having yet recovered from the effect of that day's contest. In several places we counted over fifty bullets in a single tree and thought we should have preferred some other spot if we had been a sharpshooter [in that tree]. Seven large trees had holes completely through them, made by the solid shot of artillery. The tract, which was a cornfield when Hooker's corps charged into it, is now blooming with a thrifty growth of clover.

From the Hagerstown Road, we struck across the fields in search of [Union General Abner] Doubleday's position, and after a ten minute's walk we found the little clump of trees, the stone wall, and Virginia fence about which we had heard so much from members of his division. We then came back through the fields to the large new barn which stands in the place of the building which was filled with wounded and set on fire by bursting shell. The owner was eloquent on the subject of battle and declared that it did him good "to see the rebels so severely handled." From his house we wandered down toward the old broken stone bridge where the Ninth Corps [led by General Burnside] made such brave but unsuccessful efforts to take and hold the corn-field and hill. The marks of war have disappeared from that part of the field, and acres of waving clover border upon the creek.

The round hill which intervened between the bridge and the village and which Burnside was ordered to take is now enclosed by the walls of the [Antietam] National Cemetery [established in 1865]. But a sorry place it is. The walls are beautiful specimens of masonry and the keeper's house is a fine structure. But only in these respects does the cemetery answer the descriptions given of it at the time of its dedication. Within the walls is nothing but ruin and neglect. The graves are trodden down, and the old headboards are broken and scattered. The flag staff is nothing but a fence pole bent nearly double and never supporting a flag. Rubbish covers the place where flower-beds should be; tall weeds, brush, briars, and nettles entangle the feet of the visitor at every turn. A more desolate, dreary, uncomfortable place we have not visited anywhere in the South. No cemetery have we seen that had not some care or did not show some signs of respect for the dead, except this.

It gave us the greater pain as we studied the record and found out the regiments from our own State whose representatives slept there. The 2d, 15th, 18th, 21st, 19th, 20th, 28th, 22d, 12th, 29th, 13th, and 9th [Massachusetts Infantry Regiments] have members sleeping in that desolate place. We say it is a shame to the States that undertook, with such a splurge, to make a splendid cemetery that would be a credit to this great land and then abandon it to weeds and thieves. "The paths of glory lead but to the grave" [Thomas Gray, "An Elegy Written in a Country Churchyard."], but not always to such graves as these. [The dead there number 4,684 of which 1,829 are unknown.]

When we had seen the whole field and had noted the changes in landscape, field, and dwelling since [Union General Oliver O.] Howard, [General James B.] Ricketts, Doubleday, Burnside, [General Winfield S.] Hancock, [John] Sedgwick, and Hooker made their names immortal, we called for our team and started for [nearby] South Mountain. To describe the rocky, woody eminence [at the northern end of the Blue Ridge] on which was fought [on September 14, 1862] the Battle of South Mountain [a preliminary to the Battle of Antietam] would be a difficult task indeed. However, there can have been but few changes since that day when [Union

General Orlando] Willcox, [General Samuel] Sturgis, [General Jesse L.] Reno, [General Isaac P.] Rodman, Doubleday, Ricketts, [General George G.] Meade, and Hooker defeated the enemy and dashed the exultant hopes of the Confederacy. The mountain is covered by a forest and a thick growth of underbrush through which the roads wind as curiously now as then.

GETTYSBURG

After visiting two score of battle-fields and listening to the thousand and one tales of blood and terror which the enthusiastic eulogists of each field have told us about life, valor, blood, death, and bleaching bones, we have become callous to the sentiment and enthusiasm which our first field excited. But Gettysburg, Pennsylvania, with its shot-ploughed fields and bullet-battered rocks—with its broken tree-tops and shattered fences, beside which the mound of the soldier still blooms and fades—calls up all the retiring host of patriotic emotions which deeds of bravery, martyrs' death beds, with final victory, can awaken. To us in the gathering twilight of that mellow evening the spirits of the long since dead—the faces years ago known [and loved] and since forgotten, the spectre forms of the endeared soldiers clad in Union blue and girt about with national armor—came from the woods, meadows, hills, and fields at the involuntary call of our imagination as they came from the gory [battle] fields of Bannockburn and Culloden [both in Scotland] at the call of the Highland Seer.

The long dull lines of infantry stretching from hill to hill—the bright-armed cavalry in the fields at the South, the gloomy, ominous rows of light artillery, all came again and took their stations in the fields, on the hills, and among the trees. At Wolf Hill the dusty, begrimed faces of [Union General Henry W.] Slocum's [12th Corps] men seemed to lie as they lay that 3d of July [1863], hugging the earth and firing at intervals into the woods before them. At Culp's Hill [Union General James S.] Wadsworth, [General John W.] Geary, [General Alpheus S.] Williams, and Slocum again drew up their lines and again ordered an advance.

How the woods rang! The yells, the rattle, the boom-boom, the fiery flash, the smoky cloud, the crash of bullet-cut timber, the bugle calls, and commanding shouts came from the thick grove as they came that fatal day. Besmeared and bloody faces, torn and dirty uniforms, broken bayonets, and bare heads flitted about from tree to tree, getting a shot at the foe. The dark ranks of the line of battle, some throwing up dirt and logs to form a low breastwork while the others filled the woods with searing lead, worked as diligently in the twilight as they did the night of July 2d, '63.

Then to Cemetery Hill we went, but the patriot army was there before us. [Union General] Howard rode the same sweat-streaming horse, the artillery were working the same dark cannon; the infantry lay behind the same stone wall; while down in the valley were the shifting files of [Confederate General] Early's iron-gray division. How they yelled and shrieked as they came charging across the valley, up the hillside, and over the walls! Hand to hand, gunrammer and sponge against bayonets and swords.

"Spike the guns! Surrender!" shout the rebels.

"Never! Down with rebels!" reply the artillerymen as the troops from [Union General] Hancock come to their support.

The fierce, short battle is soon decided; the rebels flee; and the brave artillerymen send their shot and whizzing shell after the broken ranks of the defeated foe. "Bang! bang!" roar on the guns. "Huzzah! huzzah!" shout on the men, as we hurry over the broken and scattered gravestones of the cemetery to Hancock's and [Union General John] Sedgwick's divisions.

There they are, just as they were that day! Massachusetts is represented in those dusty ranks that stretch along the side of the hill, down by the fence, beyond that clump of trees, and on toward Little Round Top. How firm they stand; how rapidly they fire; how patiently they wait the coming foe that is just appearing beyond the open fields; how silently they lift their pieces; how suddenly the storm breaks. How like demons [Confederate General George E.] Pickett's rebel lines shriek

and gibber on, or how like wheat before the hail-
storm they fall,then falter,then flee; while Seminary [Ridge] sends back the echo of victorious
shouts! Let them fight on through the dreary,
sleepless hours that come, while we hurry on [in
our imagination] by the ammunition wagons and
through the city of ambulances and stretchers to
the deadly hill of Little Round Top.

Here they are again—the fearless men of [Union
General Daniel E.] Sickles's and [General George]
Sykes's divisions. Here is the battery of artillery, planted in among this almost insurmountable
pile of cragged rocks, bellowing in its fury and
spitting death and terror from its fiery, Hydra
mouths. Here are the sharpshooters, creeping into
little niches in the rocks, pushing their rifles
through natural loopholes,and answering the death-
dealing shots of the rebels across the ravine at
the haggard, rocky Devil's Den. Here is the infantry line endeavoring to build a wall to protect
themselves from the hissing missiles which come
from the Peach Orchard like hail before a hurricane.

Here we can see the whole field, from the Orchard around to Culp's Hill. A cloud of smoke
covers the front lines, but in the rear are the
hurrying stretchers,the hospital colors, the lum-
bering ambulances, the reserves, and supports; all
shifting, running, stopping, changing front, lying down, leaping up, bewildering the eye; while
the tremble of the heavy guns,the clatter of wagons, the roar of musketry, and the blood-chilling
whoop of the horrid shell deafen and benumb the
ear. He that has seen the Battle of Gettysburg
will never see the like again!

Dead faces! How they haunt us! Lying all about
the fields and beside every tree in the woods. Who
are they? Whose father, or brother, or husband?
Here is a body all broken and mangled. Who praised
the symmetry of that form when last it stood in its
native Northern village? Here is a face all black
and swollen. Who was it that a few months ago
called it beautiful? Here, too, are the wounded.
The house, the yard, the adjoining field are full
of them. Over these are the surgeons. [One, in
the "butcher's barn," calls out:]

"Here, bring that man here. We have no time to examine wounds. We can cut off his leg quicker than we can dress the wound. Bring him along; don't mind his pleading. Lay him on the table. Hold on there, steward."

In slashes the knife; harsh grates the saw; and our brother or father is maimed for life. Oh! the crippled ones of battle—living a whole life of perpetual martyrdom! He that is shot and dies deserves a glorious name, but what do they not deserve who are shot and suffer a lifetime before they die?

But let these scenes of battle, like the apparitions they call up,glide into oblivion while we contemplate Gettysburg and its environs by the calm and clear daylight of peace.

The town of Gettysburg is now enjoying an era of prosperity which, but for the battle, it would never have seen. Its hotels are filled with visitors, many of whom like the beautiful valley so well that they will come and settle, bringing with them manufactories, improvements in farming, schools, and colleges that the slow, one-cent natives would never have known. The [Pennsylvania— later Gettysburg] College buildings—a hospital at the time of the battle—are now filled with hearty, intelligent students. The [Lutheran Theological] Seminary [also a hospital then] has been cleaned and repaired. A hotel has been erected at the mineral springs,and business of every kind is flourishing. But everywhere around the town the scars of battle remain.

On Seminary Ridge the trees and fences are shattered and riddled, showing plainly how fierce was the contest where the fight began. Here we found two bullets,one driven into the other so far that they could not be pulled apart. The supposition is that Union and rebel sharpshooters aimed so accurately for each other and fired at so near the same time that the bullets met, and one being a little more dense than the other pierced the one coming from the opposite direction. When we spoke of this curiosity at the hotel a whole army of relic speculators wished to purchase it. Doubtless the sum which we received for it was trebled when sold to the memento seekers who frequent the town.

These speculators do a thriving business in the relic line and have everything to sell from a 100-pound shell to the smallest wares of the toy shop, all in some way connected with the battle.

Canes cut from Culp's Hill or Little Round Top are for sale in many shop windows, and if the purchaser is a little incredulous and inclined to doubt that the canes came from those places, they will march out with him, take any sapling he may select and make it into a cane in a remarkably short time. This business has become one of great importance to Gettysburg, and it is proposed to introduce machinery for the manufacture of toys from the battle-field wood.

The traces of the fight along the front of Hancock's and Sedgwick's line—except in the blasted Peach Orchard—were not very distinct, owing to the growing fields of grain and the repairs which have been put upon the few farm houses. But the graves of the rebel dead are there, dotting the fields for miles around, generally covered with clover.

At Little Round Top the bullet scars are still visible on the rocks, while several large flat stones near which officers were killed have been engraved with their names and the dates of their deaths. The stone wall which the troops threw up as a breastwork is still entire, and the trees have not yet outgrown their wounds.

At Culp's Hill our guide pointed out to us the stumps of large trees which were cut down by the continuous fire of musketry, and a long trench in which, according to an inscription on an adjoining tree, sixty Confederates were buried. The breastwork of logs, as well as the trees which lie around, has been pulled to pieces and hacked in every way to get at the tons of bullets which the army left in them. When we were there the axes of the lead and relic hunters made the woods chipper in every direction.

On Cemetery Hill, on the opposite side of the road from the cemetery, the remains of the earth works where the heavy guns were mounted are still visible, while the stone walls at the foot of the hill remain as old and moss-covered as they were at the time those fearful charges were made over them. The arched gateway of the cemetery has been repaired,but the fearful havoc which the shot made with it can easily be imagined by the visitor who scrutinizes the variegated patches that adorn its front. The cemetery has been kept in a neat condition, the grass being often cut and the flowers by the graves braced and trimmed.

When we returned to our room at night with our mind filled with the incidents of the battle which we had heard that day and others we had listened to in other States,we could not fail to see a remarkable similarity between the battle-field of Gettysburg and the field of Waterloo [in Belgium]. Many of the charges made by the Confederates were similar in their character and result to those made by the French and were made over ravines and up hillsides which were the counterparts of those at Waterloo. [The farm of] La Haye Sainte and [the Chateau] of Hougoumont have their positions on the field of Gettysburg,although no villages mark the locations here. Pickett's last charge has often,by the best historians, been placed in the same catalogue with the [six thousand-bayonet] charge of the Old Guard at Waterloo.

In its consequences the Battle of Gettysburg may be counted as important as [the June 18,1815, Battle of] Waterloo. The former destroyed the power of a well-disciplined and defiant army which invaded the North for the express purpose of spreading desolation and ruin and, by the [eventual planned] capture of Baltimore and Washington,dictating disgraceful terms of peace, terms which would have dashed at once all the hopes entertained by lovers of republics and by the supporters of free government everywhere. Napoleon would have established a tyranny at once destructive of the interests of the people and governments of European nations. Lee would have established a slaveholding oligarchy or a monarchy,carrying the cause of humanity back into the centuries long past and annihilating the glorious work of the world's greatest and best man. Gettysburg to Lee, like Waterloo to Napoleon, was a decisive defeat. From that time, as [Confederate] General Hood declared to us not many days ago [in New Orleans],he [Lee] fought "only to save his honor."

ARMY COOKS

The history of the war is far from being written
yet! The stories are not all told. How often have
we recalled,as we have peered [during these trav-
els] into the falling cook-houses or rickety mess-
barracks,how we used to see a little company seated around the table after dinner telling stories.
"Camp stories" they were called then,although they
usually related to something funny in time of
peace. We went out to visit old Camp [Meigs] at
Readville [Massachusetts] yesterday. The old barracks remain as they were during the war [when we
were mustered in there in the summer of 1863], except where mischievous boys have pulled down the
doors or chimneys. The parade ground has changed
somewhat, as the weeds spring up from its untrod
soil. But no building of the whole camp interest-
ed us like the old, dingy, smoke-begrimed cook-
house. How we wished, as we gazed in at its open
doorway,that we might see the same line of men we
used to see and hear again the jokes they cracked
while waiting for their rations. But the majority
of them are as silent now as the old cook-house.
Some few remain to tell over the old jokes and
frighten their children with stories of war.
A little boy in Brookline [Massachusetts], whose
acquaintance we made by the roadside last week,
proudly rehearsed the deeds of his father and in
answer to our query related the same "joke of the
cook-house" in Readville, saying that it was the
only good time his father ever had. We supposed
that these jokes had been forgotten. But it seems
that men are the same to-day that they were seventy years ago. They "shoulder their crutches and
show how fields were won" [Variation of a line in
Oliver Goldsmith's "The Deserted Village."] in the
Civil War,as their grandfathers did of Revolutionary [War] battles. Many a child will this night
entreat his father or grandfather to tell him
stories of the war and after listening to fearful
tales will go to his little couch to lie awake for
hours in silent tremor or dream of guns and fero-
cious rebels.
When we were searching for the line of the [May
5-6,1864] Battle in the Wilderness [west of Fred-

ericksburg, Virginia], we found an old shanty made of the thin splinters of pine logs. It was in the corner of a little open tract of land about one-fourth of a mile back of the old Wilderness Tavern stand [forest or growth of trees]. It had a wide fireplace and a tall chimney made of mud and [wood] splinters. It had evidently never been disturbed since our army was there and was undoubtedly built the day before the battle. In it were mouldy beans, an almost empty hard-tack box, and three or four camp kettles. One of the kettles hung on a stick over the fireplace, and evidently was full of meat when left behind. All were rusty, and some had large holes through the sides. But they had never been moved after the cook had fled leaving the camp equipage of his company behind.

We have often thought of it since and conjectured what remarks that cook heard after his hasty retreat. His "masterly retreat from the cook-house at the Wilderness fight"; his "strategic movement"; his "coolness under fire"; his "faithfulness" in guarding the company's property; his having "taken a chunk of salt horse in his hat and leaving that belonging to the boys to burn"; his "breastwork of potatoes, behind which he defeated the rebs with beans at short range." Where were the sugar and the coffee he carried off on his shoulder? Couldn't he "do the skedaddling" for the whole regiment! Now, we know nothing about the history of this cook-house or the bravery of the cook; but we feel sure that, if these lines come under the eye of one "who was thar," he will say the men used just these expressions.

Cooks, under any circumstances, were an abused class of men, and especially was this the case if they lost any of the property belonging to the company. One of our acquaintances, who was a cook, is publishing a little book entitled *Army Life as a Cook;* and it will, if true to life, be a very funny book. Poor fellows! they couldn't cook like our grandmothers, hence they were abused. They were not as neat as our mothers, hence they were called slovenly. They were not as pretty as our wives, hence they were often reminded of their homeliness. But if we wished to collect the jokes, games, and tales which were common in the army, we should seek out the company cooks in preference to all others.

LESSONS OF WAR

Comrades! We must not forget the lessons taught us by war. Let romance-writers and readers or "civil backers" of rebellion cry,"We've had enough of war stories and speeches!" but it must not move the heart of the soldier. Silly tales of battle and camp, written for amusement and to swell the number of ten-cent novels,are not the war stories to which we refer. But the friends you lost, the sacrifices you made,the hardships you endured,the battles you fought, with the incidents which the memory of that strife recalls, must never be forgotten.

Rather forget that you live than forget that the past was won with a sacrifice. Tell your children of war. Tell them where you were and what you did; and what it was all for. "Shoulder your crutches and show how fields were won," telling your listeners that without the greatest vigilance they, too, must fight, and suffer, and die. Don't fraternize with the enemies of your country. Your patriotism and heroism have cost you too much. Don't lead the next generation to think that you "fought for pay" by exhibiting no patriotism now. No, comrades,when we lie down beside our fellows gone before, let our friends feel that while the soldiers lived there were not wanting voices to oppose slavery in every form or votes to defeat any measure tending toward disunion. [As American orator Wendell Phillips said in 1852:] "Eternal vigilance is the price of liberty."

"The poor we have always with us" [Variation of John 12:8.]. The maimed and the crippled ones of war are with us still,and while we live there must be hands to lift them when they fall,food for them when [they are] hungry, and friendly fingers to smooth their pillows in their lonely hours of suffering. For this purpose the Grand Army of the Republic was formed and to it should belong every sympathizing soldier of the war. [The GAR was founded in 1866 and by 1890, its peak year, had more than four hundred thousand members. Almost fanatically it promoted pensions and other benefits for the Union veterans. In 1868 Conwell was inspector general of the GAR for Minnesota.]

"We spend our years as a tale that is told," says

the psalmist [Psalm 90:9.] and doubtless since we
began these letters many a reader and many a soldier has gone down "the pathway of the ghosts and
shadows" [Henry W. Longfellow, "Hiawatha's Childhood."] leaving our numbers so many the less. Soon,
unless we,by example and work, make an impression
upon the coming generation, the war we have seen
will have been forgotten. Its trenches, redoubts,
and rifle-pits are fast disappearing;its barracks
and tents are mouldering into earth; its wounded
trees are fast healing; and even the headboards
and fences of the National cemeteries are decaying. In twenty years, like a story that is told,
the war will have left no trace to recall the scenes
so familiar now, and we of to-day will live only
in history.